WRITTEN BY LAUREN HOLOWATY

ILLUSTRATED BY MARTINA MOTZO

EDITED BY GARY PANTON

DESIGNED BY ZOE BRADLEY

COVER DESIGNED BY JOHN BIGWOOD

365 COOL WAYS to REMEMBER STUFF

Buster Books

First published in Great Britain in 2022 by Buster Books,
an imprint of Michael O'Mara Books Limited,
9 Lion Yard, Tremadoc Road, London SW4 7NQ

 www.mombooks.com/buster

 Buster Books

 @BusterBooks

 @buster_books

A CIP catalogue record for this book is available from the British Library.

ISBN: 978-1-78055-820-2

2 4 6 8 10 9 7 5 3 1

Papers used by Buster Books are natural, recyclable products made of wood
from well-managed, FSC®-certified forests and other controlled sources. The manufacturing
processes conform to the environmental regulations of the country of origin.

Printed and bound in April 2022 by CPI Group (UK) Ltd,
108 Beddington Lane, Croydon, CR0 4YY, United Kingdom

CONTENTS

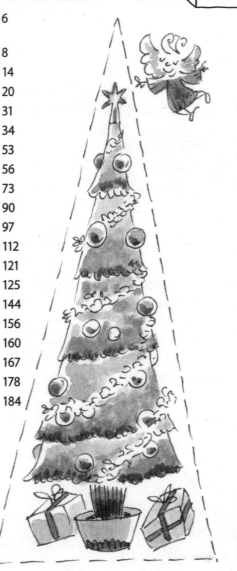

INTRODUCTION

**Your memory is amazing – and you're
about to make it even better!**

Packed into this book are 365 cool tips, shortcuts and techniques for remembering all sorts of tricky information. That amounts to one brilliant memory trick a day for an entire year.

Among the methods you'll come across are fun rhymes you can learn, simple stories that will stick in your head and even physical tricks to jog your memory. The illustrations you'll see throughout the book have been created especially to help you bring all those tough-to-remember facts to mind.

Inside you'll find ways to remember difficult spellings, times tables and dates from history, as well as pointers to help out with science, music, biology and loads of other subjects.

**So, what are you waiting for? It's time to become a
memory master!**

Take note

People remember different things in different ways, which is why some of the entries suggest more than one way of remembering the same information. It's also why some spare 'Notes' pages have been provided at the back of this book (pages 178–183). If you want to come up with any of your own rhymes, mnemonics or other memory tricks, this is where you can scribble them down.

MEMORY TRICKS AND HOW TO USE THEM

Ways to remember anything,
and how these ways work.

RHYMES AND SONGS

Have you ever noticed how easily melodies and rhymes can get stuck in your head?

Of course, some repetitive songs can be a little annoying. Does the 'Baby Shark' song drive you crazy? However, songs can also be a fantastic way of helping you to recall the important things.

There are rhymes for remembering historical dates, how to spell tricky words and even how many days there are in every month of the year (see page 56–57).

So ...

To keep your brain strong,
Just learn the song,
And you won't go wrong!

NUMBER RHYMES

If you have a long list of things to keep in mind, number-rhyming can really come in handy. Say you're packing for a holiday and you need to remember to bring ten important things. Firstly, think of ten words that rhyme with the numbers from one to ten. You could do something like this:

One = Sun
Two = Blue
Three = Knee
Four = Floor
Five = Dive
Six = Licks
Seven = Heaven
Eight = Skate
Nine = Shine
Ten = Hen

Next, imagine each of the numbers linked to one of the items you need to remember. For example, if a hat is first on your list, imagine the Sun wearing a big silly hat.

If glasses are number two (blue) on your list, think of someone wearing a very fancy pair of blue glasses.

Give it a go

Try coming up with a list of ten things that you'd want to take on holiday, and see if number-rhyming works for you. The sillier the scene you create, the more memorable it will be.

ACROSTICS

Acrostics use the first letter of each word or line to spell out a new word or message. They're really useful for remembering things that follow a certain order, such as the colours of a rainbow:

Richard **O**f **Y**ork **G**ave **B**attle **I**n **V**ain reminds you that the colours are **R**ed, **O**range, **Y**ellow, **G**reen, **B**lue, **I**ndigo, **V**iolet.

Acrostics can also be super-helpful for remembering how to spell tricky words (see the tip for how to spell the word 'beautiful' on page 36, for example).

ACRONYMS

Acronyms are words formed from the first letters of the words in a name or phrase. Acronyms are normally used to shorten and simplify names or phrases that are too long and difficult to write down or say in conversation.

For example, if you were chatting about space, you probably wouldn't say the **N**ational **A**eronautics and **S**pace **A**dministration. You'd be much more likely to use the acronym **NASA**.

Acronyms are also incredibly useful for remembering things. To see examples in this book, check out **BAT SWAB** on page 25 and **BODMAS** on pages 142–143.

STORIES

It's often more easy to remember a story than a long list of facts. Making up tales about things you need to recall can really help details to stay with you. An example of this can be found on pages 86–87, where a story has been created using parts of the names of South American capital cities, so that you can travel across a map in your mind as you read through the account. Remembering a long list of place names can be tricky, but a story with words that sound similar to the locations may be easier to recall.

GROUPING

Sometimes it can feel like there is just too much information to remember. Grouping certain things together can help you to break down a lot of information into smaller chunks that are easier for your brain to handle.

You'll find some examples of grouping when reading about the American state capitals on pages 83–85.

PICTURES

Creating pictures in your mind or drawing them on paper has a powerful influence on your memory. For example, you're less likely to forget the Spanish word for the month of May (*mayo*) if you think of an image of a calendar with mayonnaise spilt all over it!

Many of the pictures in this book work in exactly the same way.

WORD PLAY

Playing around with words and their spellings can really help with remembering facts and tricky spellings. For example, the tip on page 43 suggests that the word 'island' is easier to spell if you just remember than an island 'is land'.

PHYSICAL AIDS

It's not just your brain you have at your disposal when it comes to remembering things. You can also use parts of your body. See page 57 for an example of a way to use your own hands to help you remember how many days there are in each month of the year.

MEMORY PALACE

Your imagination is incredibly powerful, so why not use that power to help you remember things? A memory palace is a building that you can imagine and wander through inside your mind.

What to do

First, choose a place that you know well. It could be your home, or school, or any other place that you can 'walk' around easily in your mind. This is your memory palace.

Next, plan a route through your palace and follow the same directions every time you go to it. If your palace is the place where you live, you could go through the front door, down the hallway, into the living room and then the kitchen.

All that matters is that it makes sense to you and you can use the same route in your mind each time. Always going the same way will help you when it comes to remembering information in the right order.

Once you know your route, you can start storing the things you want to remember in your palace. Now, visualize each thing stored in a different area. It's helpful to make the pictures in your mind as silly as possible. The funnier they are, the more likely they are to stick in your head.

For example, if you're always forgetting birthdays you can use your memory palace to help. Let's say you need to remember that your Uncle Jack's birthday is on 1st March.

First, visualize Uncle Jack and make a mental note of any distinguishing features he has. Perhaps he has a football-shaped face and hairy nostrils, and the first object in the first room of your palace is a cupboard. Go to the cupboard in your mind and open the door to find a football with hairy nostrils *march*ing along inside, wearing a rosette with '1st' on it.

Next time you go to your palace, you will look in the cupboard and remember that Uncle Jack's birthday is on 1st March.

Why does it work?

Human brains tend to remember sensory and emotional information more easily than other things. Basically, the more meaningful something is to you, the more likely you are to remember it.

PERFECT PUNCTUATION

Ways to remember all those signs and symbols
that give meaning to your writing.

FULL STOPS

A full stop is used at the end of a sentence. In the USA and Canada,
a full stop is called a 'period'. Here are four ways to help you to
remember when to use a full stop.

Stop 1

A full stop brings a sentence to a **STOP**.

Stop 2

When your sentence is full, a full stop **stops** any more words
from getting in.

Stop 3

If you spot a full stop in the middle of a sentence, **stop** and think
about why it's there. Full stops can be used to separate letters in
abbreviations. For example, *P.T.O.* is an abbreviation of *P*lease
*T*urn *O*ver.

Stop 4

Some full stops are there to **stop** you from forgetting that a word
has been shortened. 'Prof.' is short for 'Professor', for example.

EXCLAMATION MARKS

If your statement is exciting, dramatic or loud (maybe you want to say *Ouch!* or *Run!* or *Help!*), then you can end it with an exclamation mark rather than a full stop ... like this!

Rhyme time

Remember this rhyme to help you know when to use an exclamation mark:

If it's time to shout,
Get your exclamation mark out!

> ### Did you know?
> Exclamation marks should always appear alone. Try not to get carried away by adding more!!!!!!

QUESTION MARKS

What's that you ask? When should you use a question mark? The answer is simple: use a **question** mark whenever you ask a **question**.

How to remember

Just look at your sentence and ask yourself:

Have I asked a question?
Do I need a question mark?

Here's another way of thinking about it:

When you are looking at the end of a sentence, you are on a **quest** for **qu**estion marks, **e**xclamation marks and full **st**ops. Decide which one you need, add it and your quest is complete.

COMMAS

If you're writing a list or simply adding a pause to a sentence, commas come in very handy. When you have one sentence that has two or more parts that could be separate sentences, then you need to use a comma. These parts are called clauses.

For example, this one sentence uses a comma to separate two clauses:

I like reading, so I went to the library.

Alternatively, those two clauses could be split into two separate sentences, like this:

I like reading. I went to the library.

The word that is used to join the two clauses into one sentence is 'so' and this is called a conjunction (see pages 24–26 for more on conjunctions).

Rhyme time

What's the difference between a cat and a comma?

A cat has claws at the ends of its paws,
A comma's a pause at the end of a clause.

HYPHENS AND DASHES

It's easy to confuse hyphens (-) and dashes (–), but they each have a very different job.

Hyphens (-) are shorter and they join words together. For example:

Carla's house has a ruby-red front door.

Dashes (–) are longer and separate two parts of a sentence. For example:

Our new puppy ate my slipper – he needs more training.

How to remember
*Hyphens **h**ang words together – **d**ashes **d**ivide them.*

SEMICOLONS

If you ever feel like you're writing the word 'and' too much, a semicolon (;) could be the punctuation for you. Semicolons are a great way to link up two clauses. For example:

I went to the fair with Dwight and we went on every single ride; by the time we'd finished, it was late and we were hungry.

How to remember

*A semicolon's h**and**y when **and** has been banned.*

COLONS

When you want to explain more about something or add a list into your sentence, you can use a colon (:). For example:

Anya made a list of possible names for her new pet tortoise: Pebbles, Tortellini, Turbo, Candy and Brittany.

A colon can also be used when you need to add more information to the first part of your sentence. For example:

Anya had left something behind at the pet store: her new tortoise.

How to remember

Try thinking of a colon as an *explanation* mark.

APOSTROPHES

Apostrophes (') are used to show when something belongs to something else. They are added to the ends of words and usually followed by an *s*. For example:

Martina's dog chased after Kaylee's football.

However, if the word you have is plural (which means there's more than one of something), then the apostrophe goes *after* the letter 's'. So, if Martina's dog chased after a football that belonged to a group of girls instead of just Kaylee, you would write:

Martina's dog chased after the girls' football.

Rhyme time

Add the apostrophe and then an 's',
To show that something is possessed.
If the thing has an 's' at the end,
First comes 's' then our apostrophe friend.

Other uses

Apostrophes are also used when letters have been missed out. For example:

Don't chase the ball, Frida!

In this example, *don't* stands for *do not* and the apostrophe represents the missing letter *o*.

In the same way:
It is becomes *It's.*
I am becomes *I'm.*
They are becomes *They're.*

How to remember

*A**po**strophes show **p**ossession and **o**mission.*

EXCELLENT ENGLISH

Ways to remember the trickiest
parts of the English language.

THE ALPHABET

Remembering the letters of the alphabet is as easy as A, B, C! If you know the nursery rhyme 'Twinkle, Twinkle, Little Star', then it's easy to sing the alphabet to the same tune.

A B C D E F G,

(Twinkle, twinkle, little star,)

H I J K L M N O P,

(How I wonder what you are.)

Q R S T U V,

(Up above the world so high,)

W X Y and Z.

(Like a diamond in the sky.)

Now I know my ABCs,

(Twinkle, twinkle, little star,)

Next time won't you sing with me?

(How I wonder what you are.)

VOWELS AND CONSONANTS

There are 26 letters in the English alphabet. Five of the letters are vowels, which are soft sounds. The five vowels are A, E, I, O and U. The remaining 21 letters are consonants.

How to remember

You can use a simple acrostic such as the one below to help you to remember the vowels.

An Eagle Is Over Us

This will also help you to learn the order that the vowels come in the alphabet.

To remember that vowels are soft sounds, try thinking of this:

*The **owl** in v**owel** hoots softly.*

NOUNS

A noun is any name of a person, animal, object, thing, place or idea. All of the words underlined in the sentence below are examples of nouns:

Sam, Moesha and their dog Woofles live in a little house in the city of Leeds.

How to remember

*A **n**oun is a **n**ame.*

Did you know?

'Proper nouns' are names that start with a capital letter, such as the names of people, towns and countries. In the example on the left, which nouns do you think are proper nouns? The answer is at the bottom of the next page.

21

ADJECTIVES

Adjectives describe nouns by giving more information about them. They can say what feeling, colour, size, shape, taste, texture, smell, number or sound the noun has. Adjectives usually go in front of nouns. The words underlined in the sentence below are examples of adjectives:

The <u>brave</u> cat pounced on the <u>smelly</u> slipper.

How to remember

Adjectives **add** more information.

Give it a go

Another good way to remember what adjectives are is to think of a list of adjectives whose first letters spell out the word 'ADJECTIVE'. Here's one example below:

Adjectives are:

Adventurous

Delicious

Jolly

Energetic

Clever

Terrific

Important

Valuable

Excellent

See if you can come up with your own list of adjectives that spells out the word 'ADJECTIVE'. You can use the Notes section at the back of the book to write them down.

The proper nouns on the previous page are Sam, Moesha, Woofles and Leeds.

VERBS

Verbs are doing and being words. They describe the action in a sentence. The words underlined in the sentence below are all verbs:

Rachel <u>climbs</u>, <u>runs</u> and <u>jumps</u>.

Give it a go

The words in this list are all verbs and they spell out the word 'VERB'. Can you come up with a list of your own?

Vanish

Escape

Run

Bolt

AUXILIARY VERBS

Sometimes, verbs need to be more descriptive. That's where auxiliary verbs such as 'to be', 'to have', 'to do' and 'will be' come in handy. The underlined words in the sentences below are auxiliary verbs:

Rachel <u>has been</u> climbing.

Rachel <u>will be</u> running.

Rachel <u>does not</u> like jumping.

How to remember

*An au**x**iliary verb gives a verb e**x**tra help.*

ADVERBS

Adverbs describe verbs by adding more information to them. They often end in the letters 'ly' (but not always). The underlined word in the next sentence is an adverb:

Declan <u>silently</u> crept.

Adverbs can show what, why, when, how and where things are done. The underlined words below show some more examples of adverbs:

<u>Sometimes</u>, Declan <u>silently</u> creeps <u>around</u> the room, <u>barely</u> making a sound.

How to remember

*An **ad**verb useful**ly ad**ds information to a verb.*

Give it a go

Can you make your own list of words whose initial letters spell out the word 'ADVERB'? Here's an example:

Accidentally	**D**reamily	**V**aliantly
Eagerly	**R**arely	**B**adly

CONJUNCTIONS

Conjunctions are used to join two sentences or phrases together. Words such as 'and', 'or' and 'but' are conjunctions. The conjunction in the sentence below has been underlined.

Sameer enjoys watching basketball, <u>but</u> he doesn't like playing it.

How to remember

*Con**junction**s are used at the **junction** where two sentences meet.*

To remember some common conjunctions, just think of 'FANBOYS'.

For

And

Nor

But

Or

Yet

So

SUBORDINATING CONJUNCTIONS

Subordinating conjunctions join one part of a sentence, which would make sense on its own, to another sentence that wouldn't make sense on its own. The underlined word in the sentence below is a subordinating conjunction:

Sameer plays basketball <u>because</u> he has to.

How to remember

To remember some of the most common subordinating conjunctions, you just need to think of one thing: 'BAT SWAB'.

Before

After

Though

So

While

As

Because

CORRELATIVE CONJUNCTIONS

Correlative conjunctions are conjunctions that always come in a pair. The two words underlined below are correlative conjunctions:

Ben wasn't <u>as</u> good at bird spotting <u>as</u> Ann.

How to remember

Keep in mind those names 'BEN' and 'ANN' because they can help you to remember the most common correlative conjunctions.

'Both' goes with 'and'

'Either' goes with 'or'

'Neither' goes with 'nor'

'As' goes with 'as'

'Not only' goes with 'but also'

'Not' goes with 'but'

PREFIXES

Prefixes are letters that are added to the beginning of a word and usually change that word's meaning. For example, if you put the prefix 'dis' before 'liked' it makes 'disliked', meaning the opposite of 'liked'. If you put the prefix 're' in front of 'fresh' it becomes 'refresh', meaning 'to make fresh again'.

In the sentence below, the prefixes are underlined:

Clara <u>dis</u>liked her new <u>anti</u>gravity boots.

How to remember

You can learn common prefixes in your sleep! Just remember the word 'DREAM':

*'**D**is' gives the word its opposite meaning ('dis' + 'like' = 'dislike')*

*'**R**e' means 'again' ('re' + 'visit' = 'revisit')*

*'**E**x' means 'former' ('ex' + 'president' = 'ex-president')*

*'**A**nti' means 'against' ('anti' + 'freeze' = 'antifreeze')*

*'**M**is' means 'wrongly' ('mis' + 'understand' = 'misunderstand')*

Did you know?
The prefix 'pre' means 'before', so the word 'prefix' tells you that it comes *before* a word.

SUFFIXES

Suffixes are added to the ends of words and can change their meanings. For example, if you add the suffix 'less' to the word 'hope' you get the word 'hopeless' – which is the opposite of having 'hope'.

Suffixes can also change how a word is used. For example, adding the suffix 'ly' to the end of the adjective 'slow' makes the word 'slowly'. In this case, the meaning of 'slow' hasn't changed, but the way you would use the word has.

In the following sentence, the suffixes have been underlined:

Sloths are use<u>less</u> in races because they move so slow<u>ly</u>.

How to remember

To remember some other common suffixes, just think of 'ICE TEA'.

*'**I**ze' added to a noun creates a verb ('symbol' + 'ize' = 'symbolize')*

*'**C**y' combined with a noun, verb or adjective creates a noun ('urgent' + 'cy' = 'urgency')*

*'**E**ry' combined with a noun, verb or adjective makes a noun ('bake' + 'ery' = 'bakery')*

*'**T**ion' added to a noun, verb or adjective makes a noun ('act' + 'tion' = 'action')*

*'**E**nt' added to a noun, verb or adjective makes an adjective ('differ' + 'ent' = 'different')*

*'**A**ble' added to a noun or verb makes an adjective ('drink' + 'able' = 'drinkable')*

PRONOUNS

Pronouns are words such as 'she', 'he', 'you' and 'it'. You can use a pronoun when you've already used a noun (such as a person's name) once, so that you don't need to use it again. In the sentence below, the pronouns have been underlined:

Mohammed couldn't believe <u>his</u> luck when <u>he</u> won the school raffle.

How to remember
Here are two ways of remembering what pronouns are. Give them a try, and use the one that best sticks in your mind and makes the most sense to you:

I. *__Pro__nouns __pro__p up nouns when they need a rest.*

2. *A __pro__noun is a __pro__fessional noun, like a stand-in or stunt person. A real __pro__!*

PREPOSITIONS

Prepositions explain where a noun is in relation to something else. 'On', 'in', 'at', 'under', 'by', 'of', 'off', 'at', 'to' and 'into' are all examples of prepositions. The prepositions have been underlined in this sentence:

Oswald the octopus lies <u>on</u> a rock <u>in</u> a cave <u>at</u> the bottom of the ocean.

How to remember
A pre__position__ shows the noun's __position__.

INTERJECTIONS

EEK! What was that? Don't worry, it's just an interjection. Interjections are small words that can be used on their own and don't need to link to the other words before or after them. Here are a few examples:

How to remember

Interjections are used to show emotion. We'd better not forget to go **inter** that or there will be **objections**!

CAPITALIZATION

Remembering which words need capital letters can be a little confusing at times. Names and words that begin sentences are easy ones, but what about everything else?

How to remember

To know when to capitalize a word, all you need to think of is 'MINTS'.

Months, days of the week and holidays (such as Christmas and Eid)

I capitalize the letter 'I' when it's me

Names of places and people

Titles of books, movies and TV shows

Start of a sentence

FIGURES OF SPEECH

Ways to remember some of the
many quirks of the English language.

METAPHORS

A metaphor is a way of
describing something by saying
that it is something else.
For example:

Caitlyn is a walking dictionary.

Of course, this does not
mean that Caitlyn is actually
a dictionary with the power
to walk. It just means that she
knows a lot of words, so is being
compared to a dictionary.

How to remember
Recalling this phrase should
help you to remember what
a metaphor is.

*I **met a** friend **phor** lunch.
She has a heart of gold.*

Your friend doesn't actually have
a heart of gold. This is just a way
of using a metaphor to say that
she is very kind and special.

SIMILES

A simile is a way of describing something by saying that it is like something else. These two sentences contain similes:

*His eyes sparkled **like** diamonds.*

*His eyes are **as** blue **as** the sky.*

How to remember

Similes normally use 'as' or 'like' – which are other words for **simi**lar.

It may also help to think of a simile as a simi**like**.

ALLITERATION

Always **a**sking **a**bout **a**lliteration? Alliteration is when words start with the same letter or sound. Here's an example:

Busy **b**ees **b**ullied the **b**ears.

How to remember

*Alliteration is **l**ittered with **l**ots of identical **l**etters.*

ASSONANCE

Assonance is when the vowels in two or more words rhyme, but not the consonants. The words *tide*, *rises* and *find* have assonance with each other. Words also have assonance when their consonants are the same, but their vowels aren't – for example, ***mast*** and ***mist***.

How to remember

*As the tide rises, the sailors find that **most** of the **mast** is hidden by **mist**.*

ONOMATOPOEIA

When you want a word to sound like the noise it's describing, you can use onomatopoeia. Examples of onomatopoeia are words such as:

Bang. Buzz. Zoom. Boing. Slither. Whoosh. Achoo.

How to remember

Imagine yourself banging a gong – BANG! – while standing *on a mat on a pier*.

> **Did you know?**
> Onomatopoeia is pronounced 'on-oh-mat-oh-pee-ah'.

SUPER SPELLING

Ways to remember even the hardest of spellings.

ACCEPTABLE

It can be easy to forget whether *acceptable* ends with an 'able' or an 'ible'. The phrase below should help you to remember the correct way from now on:

I am **able** to **accept** that I can spell **acceptable**.

ACCIDENT

Struggling to remember the two 'c's in the middle and the 'ent' at the end of *accident*? This should help you:

When two **c**ars **c**ollide there **is** a **dent**.

ACCOMMODATE

Just remember, *accommodate* is a long word. It needs to be to *accommodate* the two 'a's, two 'o's, double 'c' and double 'm'.

ADDRESS

Notice that *address* has two sets of double letters. It may help to remember that if you want to send an email, you need to **add** the correct **add**re**ss** so it arrives **s**afe and **s**ound.

ARGUMENT

When 'argue' turns into *argument*, the 'e' is lost. Here's a way to keep that in mind:

*The **e** in argu**e** always loses in an **argument**.*

ARITHMETIC

Here's a memory trick that's as easy as 1, 2, 3. The initial letters in this phrase spell out *arithmetic*, so just remember the phrase and you'll be good to go:

***A** **r**at **i**n **t**he **h**ouse **m**ay **e**at **t**he **i**ce **c**ream.*

ASTHMA

The name of this lung condition has a 'th' in the middle, even though it's pronounced 'ass-mah'. To remember the 'th', try thinking of this phrase:

*People with as**th**ma may have trouble brea**th**ing.*

BEARD

Remember, you can't spell *beard* without 'ear':

*A b**ear**d grows from **ear** to **ear**.*

BEAUTIFUL

The first part of *beautiful* can be tricky, but the initial letters in this phrase may help:

***B**ig **e**lephants **a**ren't **u**gly, they're **beau**tiful!*

BELIEVE

Believe has 'lie' in the middle. Remember:

*You should never be**lie**ve a **lie**.*

BICYCLE

The spelling of *bicycle* can trip up even the best of spellers. Just remember:

*Never use your b**icy**cle when the road is **icy**.*

BREAKFAST

'Fast' can mean quick, but it can also mean a period of time spent without eating any food:

*After sleeping, you eat your **breakfast** and **break** your **fast**.*

BROCCOLI

Broccoli has two 'c's and one 'l', just like this phrase:

*My **bro**ther **c**an't **c**hew **or** **li**ck.*

CALENDAR

Calendar has two 'a's. A *calendar* also includes two months that start with 'A' (**A**pril and **A**ugust).

CAMPAIGN

If you *campaign* for something, you're trying to convince people to agree with you and maybe even to vote for you. Just don't forget that 'g' in the middle:

*A campai**g**n is all about **g**etting people's votes.*

COMMITTEE

A *committee* is made up of a group of people. The word *committee* also has a group of double letters: double 'm's, double 't's and double 'e's.

CONSCIENCE

Conscience is pronounced 'kon-shunns', but it's spelled very differently. It becomes much easier to spell if you think of it as two words – **con** and **science** – smashed together.

*If you smash **con** and **science** together, it might give you a guilty **conscience**.*

COULD

Could is one of the many words in the English language that contains a sneaky silent letter. To remember the ending of *could*, and also 'should' and 'would', just think:

***O**h, **u** **l**ucky **d**uck!*

DEFINITE

*There is **definite**ly no 'a' in **definite**.*

DESPERATE

Ever been *desperate* for a wee? Well, *desp**e**rate* has an 'e' in the middle, just like 'w**ee**'!

DESSERT

Dessert is another word for the sweet treat you might eat at the end of a meal. However, it's often misspelled as 'desert' (which is a large area of dry land). Remembering this phrase will help you to avoid making that mistake:

*De**ss**ert has an extra 's' for added sweetne**ss**.*

DIARRHOEA

As well as being very hard to deal with, *diarrhoea* is also hard to spell. In fact, it's probably one of the trickiest words in the English language. The initial letters of this phrase might come in useful:

Dash **i**n **a** **r**eal **r**ush, **h**urry **o**r **e**lse **a**ccident.

DIFFICULTY

Use the rhyme below and this word will no longer give you any *difficulty*:

*Mrs **D**, Mrs **I**, Mrs **F F I**,*

*Mrs **C**, Mrs **U**, Mrs **L T Y**!*

EMBARRASS

If you get *embarrass*ed, it means that something has happened to make you feel foolish, shy, awkward or ashamed – so you could say:

*Embarr**ass** ends with feeling like an **ass**.*

ENVIRONMENT

To remember the 'n' in the middle of *environment*, think of the *enviro**n**ment* being '**n**ature'.

EXAGGERATE

When you *exaggerate* something, you make it seem much bigger, smaller, better or worse than it really is. But don't *exaggerate* how difficult this word is to spell. All you have to remember is the double 'g' (pronounced as a 'j') and the 'e' in the middle:

***G**oofy **Gr**eg loves to exa**gge**rate.*

EXCELLENT

So you don't forget the 'c' in *excellent*, remember this:

*You can **c**ount on an ex**c**ellent person.*

GORGEOUS

Something can look *gorgeous*, but it could also taste *gorgeous*:

*You might **gorge** on something that is **gorge**ous.*

GOVERNMENT

Watch out for the 'n' in the middle of *government*. Just think:

*A gover**n**ment gover**n**s.*

GRAMMAR

Don't let the 'a' at the end of *grammar* catch you out. Remember:

*My grand**ma** always uses perfect gram**ma**r.*

HURRICANE

A *hurricane* is an extremely powerful wind or storm, so it makes sense that:

*If there's a **hurri**cane, **hurr**y **i**nside.*

HYMN

Hymn is an unusual word because it contains no vowels. You can remember how to spell it by using the initial letters from this phrase:

Have you made noise?

IMMEDIATELY

You can't spell *immediately* without 'media'.

*If you see someone famous, call the **media** im**media**tely.*

INTERRUPT

To remember the double 'r' in the middle of *interrupt*, think of the word as two words that have been squashed together: 'inter' (meaning 'between') and 'rupt' (short for 'rupture', meaning 'to break'). If you *interrupt* two people having a conversation, you are breaking between them.

ISLAND

Here's a very easy way to remember the silent 's' in *island*:

*An **island is land**.*

LAUGH

Laugh is one of those words with a jumble of letters that can easily get mixed up. To get them in the right order, just remember:

***L**augh and **u** **g**et **h**appy.*

LIBRARY

The initial letters in this phrase will help you with the spelling of *library*:

Living in books really aids reading years.

LOOSE

Loose often gets confused with 'lose'. *Loose* means 'free' or 'not tightly held in place', whereas 'lose' is the opposite of 'win'. Remember the difference with this phrase:

*One of the **o**'s in l**oo**se is l**oo**se, so you might l**o**se it.*

MILLIONAIRE

Millionaire has two 'l's but only one 'n', so you might say:

*A mi**ll**ionaire has **l**ots of **l**oot, but only one **n**.*

MINIATURE

Miniature means 'very small', and it also contains two very small words: 'i' and 'a'.

*Min**ia**ture.*

MINUSCULE

Minuscule is another word that means 'very small'. This tip should help you to remember the 'u' in the middle:

Minuscule *things are so small that it's almost as if they are* **minus** *something.*

MISCHIEVOUS

Mischievous is like 'mischief', but with the same ending as 'nervous':

*The mis**chievous** child is* **chie**fly ner**vous***.*

MISSPELL

When you *misspell* a word, you spell it incorrectly. This short phrase should help you to remember that it has a double 's':

Miss Pell *will never* **misspell***.*

NECESSARY

Necessary has one 'c' and a double 's', so it's just like a shirt, which has *one **c**ollar and two **s**leeves.*

OCCUR

Occur might be a short word, but the double 'c' can trip people up. Thinking of it this way may help:

*The idea of crossing two seas (**'c**'s) did not o**cc**ur to me.*

OCEAN

To avoid mixing up the letters in the middle of *ocean*, remember this phrase (and picture the image):

***O**ld **c**amels **e**at **a**mazing **n**oodles.*

PASTIME

A *pastime* is a hobby or activity that a person does for enjoyment. It sounds like 'past time', but it's just one word. Remember it with this:

Pa's time is spent on his **pastime**.

PEOPLE

The unusual 'o' in the middle of *people* can be remembered with:

People **e**at **o**melettes, **p**eople **l**ike **e**ggs.

PREJUDICE

A *prejudice* is an unfair dislike or judgement of someone or something. Remember how to spell prejudice by splitting it into two parts. *Pre* means 'before' and *judice* means 'judgement'. If you have a prejudice, you're making a judgement before you know the facts.

PRIVILEGE

Here's a hint for remembering that *privilege* ends with 'lege' rather than 'ledge':

It's a privi**lege** to have **leg**s.

PTERODACTYL

With its unusual silent 'p' at the start, spelling *pterodactyl* can be 'ptricky'. It may help to think that the 'pt' at the beginning could stand for **p**retty **t**errifying.

Alternatively, you could just think of this joke:

Why can't you hear a pterodactyl when it's in the bathroom?
Because it has a silent 'p'!

QUESTIONNAIRE

To remember the double 'n' in *questionnaire*, keep in mind this phrase:

*Her **question**s were **n**ever **aire**d.*

QUEUE

Queue can be one of the toughest words to spell. Here's a phrase to help you with the order of the last three vowels:

Q*ueen **U****rsula **e****ats **u****p **e****ggs.*

REHEARSAL

Rehearsal has 'hear' in the middle, which you can remember with this:

*At the **rehearsal**, you'll **re**ally **hear Sal**ly sing.*

RHYTHM

Memorize this phrase and you'll never lose your *rhythm* again:

R*hythm **h****elps **y****our **t****wo **h****ips **m****ove.*

SECRETARY

You can't spell *secretary* without 'secret':

*Shh! The **secret**ary knows all the boss's **secret**s!*

SEPARATE

Separate is often spelled incorrectly, usually with an 'e' in the middle where the first 'a' should be. All you need to save you from making this mistake is a rat!

*There is **a rat** in sep**arat**e.*

SINCERELY

Think of *sincerely* as 'since' and 'rely' mashed together:

***Since** I **rely** on honesty, I must say things **sincerely**.*

SPEECH

Even though 'speak' has 'ea' in the middle, *speech* has 'ee'. Remember:

*Never sn**ee**ze while making a sp**ee**ch.*

STATIONERY AND STATIONARY

One of the most common spelling mistakes is to confuse *stationery* (pens, paper and other writing equipment) with 'stationary' (not moving). Luckily, there's an easy way to tell them apart.
Just remember:

*E is for **e**nvelope, and there's an **e** in station**e**ry.*

*If you're station**a**ry, you're **a**bsolutely still.*

SUBTLE

Subtle, which means 'not immediately obvious' or 'delicate or faint', has a silent 'b' in the middle. Remember it with this:

*If you want to **b** su**b**tle, you have to **b** silent.*

SUCCEED

Succeed is one of the few words in the English language that ends in 'ceed'. Can you think of any others? You'll find two more at the bottom of the next page.

*If you use a double **c** and a double **e** you will su**cce**ed.*

TOMORROW

Memorizing this phrase will help you with spelling *tomorrow*:

*We might see **Tom or Row**ena **tomorrow**.*

TONGUE

Be careful not to confuse *tongue* (that thing in your mouth) with 'tongs' (the objects you might use for holding hot food or curling hair). To learn the spelling of *tongue*, remember the initial letters of:

***T**iny **o**wls **n**est **g**rumpily **u**nder **e**lms.*

WEIRD

You can remember how to spell *weird* with this phrase:

***We b**ir**d**s *are **weird**!*

Did you know?
You may have heard the phrase *"'I' before 'E' except after 'C'"*, but *weird* is one of several words in English that breaks this 'rule'. Other examples include 'foreign', 'height', 'seize' and 'glacier'.

YACHT

Remember this very tricky spelling with these initial letters:

***Y**ellow **a**nts **c**an't **h**ave **t**oast.*

Two other words ending in 'ceed' are 'proceed' and 'exceed'.

WRITING IT DOWN

Ways to remember the
right ways to write.

PAST, PRESENT AND FUTURE TENSE

Tenses tell you *when* an action is taking place. The present tense is
what is happening now or today. The past tense is what happened
yesterday or any time before now. The future tense is what will
happen tomorrow or any time later than now.

How to remember

Past	Present	Future
"I **pas**sed the ball in the **past**."	"I'm opening my **present**s right away."	"I look **f**orward to the **future**."

FIRST, SECOND AND THIRD PERSON

You can write in the first, second or third person – but which one is which?

First person is when the writer or speaker is the person doing something. For example: *I write*.

Second person is when the writer or speaker uses 'you'. For example: *You write*.

Third person is when the writer or speaker is referring to someone else. For example: *He writes*, *She writes* or *They write*.

How to remember

Think of yourself with a friend and their sister taking it in turns to write part of a story:

I can write **first**, **you** go **second** and **she** can go **third**.

LETTER WRITING

When you send a letter or an email to a friend or relative, you can end it whichever way you like. However, when you send a more formal letter or email, you should sign off with either 'Yours sincerely' (if you're writing to someone you have met before) or 'Yours faithfully' (if you're writing to someone you've never met).

Rhyme time

This rhyme will help you to remember when you should use each sign-off:

Since we spoke
I'm yours **since**rely,
Faithfully – we've never
met (clearly).

STORYTELLING

Want to write a story, but not sure where to begin? There are a few elements that pretty much all good stories share. If you can remember what these elements are, you stand a great chance of creating a classic!

How to remember

Think of these six famous characters. Each one represents a different element to keep in mind when writing your story.

Pocahontas   **P** is for **Plot**
Your plot is your storyline. What is your beginning, middle and end?

Cinderella   **C** is for **Characters**
The characters are the people in your story. What are your characters like? Are they humans or animals? Big or small? Male or female? Mean or kind? Heroes or villains? Great stories have lots of different types of characters.

Snow White   **S** is for **Setting**
The setting is where your story takes place. Your setting could be a castle, an alien planet, an underwater kingdom or even your own home.

Mulan   **M** is for **Mood**
Is your story happy and funny or sad and tragic?

Fiona   **F** is for **Focus**
Who are your lead characters? Pick out one or two and make them the focus of your story.

Tiana   **T** is for **Theme**
Does your story have a message to tell your reader or an issue? A theme could be friendship or family or a lesson learned by your lead character. Pick something that matters to you. It's up to you!

OUR PLANET AND BEYOND

Ways to remember the world around
you and the bits that really make it tick.

DAYS IN A MONTH

There are a few different ways of remembering how many days are
in each month of the year. Give these a try, and go with the one
that works best for you.

Rhyme time 1

This is the most common rhyme you're likely to hear for
remembering the days in a month:

Thirty days have September,
April, June and November.
All the rest have thirty-one,
Except for February alone,
And that has twenty-eight days clear,
With twenty-nine in each leap year.

Rhyme time 2

This rhyme uses the number order of the months (so 'fourth',
for example, refers to April – the fourth month of the year):

Fourth, eleventh, ninth and sixth,
Thirty days to each affix,
Every other thirty-one,
Except the second month alone.

Using a visual

Your hands can also help you to remember. Make fists with both of your hands and hold them out in front of you (as in the picture below).

Look at your knuckles and the little dips between them. Each one represents a month. The dips between each knuckle are the months that have 30 days, except for February (which has 28, or 29 in a leap year).

JANUARY
FEBRUARY
MARCH
APRIL
MAY JUNE JULY AUGUST
SEPTEMBER
OCTOBER
NOVEMBER
DECEMBER

LEAP YEARS

Most years are 365 days long, but every fourth year is a leap year. A leap year is a year made up of 366 days. This is because it takes the Earth 365.24 days to travel around the Sun. By having an extra day every four years, it balances out that extra quarter of a day. Whenever there is a leap year, the extra day is added to February, making it 29 days long instead of the usual 28.

How to remember

To remember which years are leap years, just use your four times table. In this century, the leap years are: 2000, 2004, 2008, 2012, 2016, 2020, 2024, 2028, 2032 and so on.

INTERNATIONAL TRAVEL

Have you ever gone on holiday and had to change the time on your watch? Or chatted to someone far away when it's night-time for them but daytime for you? This happens because the world is divided up into different time zones. The Sun rises in the east, which means that eastern places have daylight before western places. Without time zones, there would be locations where the Sun rises in the middle of the night!

How to remember

If you travel between times zones from east to west, you gain time because you're moving back through the day. If you travel east, you lose time. This quick phrase should help you remember how it works:

Westward gains,
Eastward wanes.

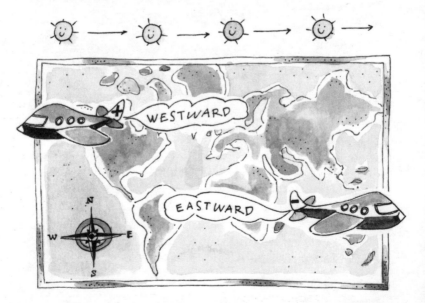

HURRICANE SEASON

The United States of America and the Caribbean have a hurricane season. This means it can be very windy between the months of June and October.

Rhyme time

These mini-rhymes will help you to remember the months of the hurricane season.

June – too soon (for the worst storms)
July – stand by (the real hurricanes are coming)
August – you must (be prepared for a battering)
September – remember (it's not finished yet)
October – all over (for another year)

HURRICANES, CYCLONES AND TYPHOONS

Hurricanes, cyclones and typhoons are violent storms with extremely high winds that start over warm seas. Their names are different because of where they are formed. For the most part, if a storm originates over the Atlantic Ocean, it's a hurricane. If it begins over the Indian Ocean, it's called a cyclone. If the storm is over the Pacific Ocean, it's a typhoon.

How to remember

This phrase should help you to group the pairs of storms and oceans together:

*If you sail the **Atlantic** in a **hurr**y,*
***Cycl**e to **India** in a flurry,*
*You'll soon grow **ti**red by the **pac**e.*

SUNRISE AND SUNSET

Although it seems as though the Sun is travelling across the sky during the day, it's actually the Earth that is moving. The Earth turns towards the east, which is why it looks like the Sun rises in the east. As your location on Earth turns away from the Sun, night-time comes.

How to remember
*The Sun rises **ea**rly in the **ea**st and sets **we**ary in the **we**st.*

CHANGING CLOCKS

All over the world there are lots of countries that change their clocks twice a year to make the most of long summer days. In Britain, summer time begins at 1 am on the last Sunday in March and ends at 2 am on the last Sunday in October. Clocks are put forward by one hour in March and turned back by one hour in October.

How to remember
In the United States, autumn is called 'fall', so you can remember which way the clocks change by thinking:

Spring forward, fall back.

If the above doesn't work for you, you could try using this phrase:

Forward March, to the end of October and back.

LAYERS OF THE EARTH

Have you ever tried digging into the ground to see how far down you can go? Just to get through the Earth's crust, you'd need to dig up to 70 km deep. If you got through that, you'd reach the mantle. This is a 2,900 km-thick layer of semi-molten rock. Then comes the outer core, which has a depth of at least 2,200 km and is made of liquid iron and nickel. In the middle is the inner core, which has a radius of 1,200 km (see page 154 to learn about radius) and made of solid iron. The inner core's temperature is at least 5,000°C. That's almost 90 times hotter than the hottest temperature ever recorded in the Sahara Desert.

Rhyme time

This rhyme will help you to remember all four layers of the Earth, from the inside out:

There's the inner and the outer core,
Then the mantle and the crust makes four.

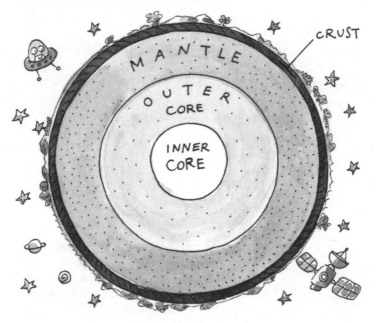

MAGMA AND LAVA

Deep under the Earth's surface, in an area called the mantle, it is so hot that rocks melt. This semi-liquid rock is called magma. When a volcano erupts, magma comes to the surface and can be seen. When this happens, the magma becomes known as lava.

How to remember

To keep in mind the difference between magma and lava, just think of this phrase:

***La**va is on **la**nd and **ma**gma is in the **ma**ntle.*

ARCTIC AND ANTARCTIC

The two coldest places on Earth are the North Pole and the South Pole (also known as the polar regions). The North Pole is the most northerly part of the planet and is called the Arctic. The South Pole is the most southerly part and is called the Antarctic.

How to remember

The **Arc**tic is at the top of the world, so think of the top of an **arc**h. The **Ant**arctic is on the opposite side of the world, the **ant**ithesis (which means the opposite of something).

> ### Did you know?
> Polar bears and penguins never meet in the wild because polar bears live in the Arctic (which is made of floating ice) while penguins live in the Antarctic (which is made of rock). To remember this, just think of a polar bear on some sea ice and a penguin jumping off an icy rock.

THE ATMOSPHERE

Earth is surrounded by layers of gases (which you probably know as 'air'). The air is made up of roughly 78 per cent nitrogen, 21 per cent oxygen and almost 1 per cent argon.

How to remember

This handy phrase uses the beginnings of the three most common gases in the Earth's atmosphere – **ni**trogen, **ox**ygen and **arg**on:

*Last **ni**ght, my smelly s**ox** caused an **arg**ument and created a bad **atmosphere**.*

SPHERES OF THE ATMOSPHERE

The higher you travel away from the surface of the Earth, the thinner the atmosphere gets until you eventually find yourself in space. Each part of the Earth's atmosphere has its own name:

Troposphere

This is the first layer of the atmosphere, reaching up 8–15 km above the Earth's surface. This is where weather occurs and aeroplanes fly.

Stratosphere

This next part of the sky is between 15 and 50 km above the Earth's surface.

Mesosphere

Meteors flash across this area, which is around 50–85 km from sea level.

Thermosphere

This is about 85–600 km up.

Exosphere

Most satellites orbit the Earth within this sphere. It stretches up for thousands of kilometres into space.

How to remember

Use this sentence to help you learn the different spheres in the correct order:

***Tro**lls who **stra**y **mes**s up **the**ir **ex**it.*

(**Tro**posphere, **stra**tosphere, **mes**osphere, **the**rmosphere, **ex**osphere.)

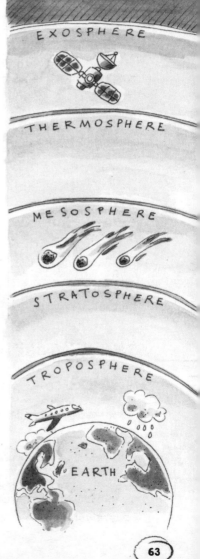

RICHTER SCALE

The Richter scale is used to measure how powerful an earthquake is. Each number on the scale represents a strength that is ten times greater than the previous number. So, for example, an earthquake measuring five on the Richter scale is ten times stronger than an earthquake measuring four.

How to remember

To remember that the **Rich**ter scale measures earthquakes, try picturing this image:

*A king loses all his **rich**es in an earthquake.*

> ### Did you know?
> The most powerful earthquake in recorded history measured 9.5 on the Richter scale. It occured in 1960, near Valdivia in Chile.

BEAUFORT SCALE

The Beaufort scale measures wind speed. On a calm day with no wind, the measurement would be zero. At the top end of the scale, measuring 12, are hurricanes with wind speeds higher than 118 km per hour.

How to remember

To remember that the Beaufort (pronounced '**bow**-fort') scale measures wind speed, imagine a girl fighting to keep a **bow** on her head in strong winds.

SAFFIR-SIMPSON SCALE

When a hurricane is so powerful that it goes beyond a 12 on the Beaufort scale (see page 64), it is measured by the Saffir–Simpson scale. This scale has categories ranging from one to five.

How to remember

To remember that the Saffir–Simpson scale measures hurricanes, think of this phrase:

A ship called the **SS Hurricane** *sailed on a* **s**tormy **s**ea.

> ### Did you know?
> One of the most powerful hurricanes ever to hit land was Hurricane Andrew in 1992. It was registered as a Category Five and reached speeds of 266 km per hour.

ENHANCED FUJITA SCALE

Tornadoes have even higher wind speeds than hurricanes, and are measured by the Enhanced Fujita Scale. The scale ranges from EF0 (up to 137 km per hour) to EF5 (over 320 km per hour).

How to remember

Fujita sounds like 'fudge-eater', so think of someone being swept up in a tornado while eating some fudge.

WATER CYCLE

Water is constantly moving from land to seas and rivers, up to the sky and back down to the land. This is called the water cycle and it has four stages: evaporation, condensation, precipitation and infiltration. The diagram below shows the water cycle in action:

Evaporation
This is when water changes into gas. An example of this is when the Sun heats up a puddle and the puddle disappears.

Infiltration
This is when water hits the ground. Some is soaked up into the ground, and some runs off the surface into rivers and lakes.

Condensation
This is when a gas changes into a liquid. An example of this is when water droplets create clouds.

Precipitation
This is when any water falls from the sky. It could be rain, snow, hail or even mist.

Rhyme time

Those four stages become much easier to understand if you memorize this poem:

*Evaporation turns water into **vap**our, a gas floating on high.*
*Con**dens**ation makes it **dens**er, clouds appear in the sky.*
*Pre**cip**itation falls as rain, in a liquid you can **sip**.*
*Then in**fil**tration **fil**ls up lakes and trickles drip by drip.*

CELSIUS AND FAHRENHEIT

Celsius and Fahrenheit are two different scales, but both are used for measuring temperature. The United States, Liberia and a small number of other countries use Fahrenheit. The rest of the world uses Celsius. Knowing the difference can come in very handy. For example, you'll want to put on your summer-wear if it's a hot and sunny 32 degrees Celsius outside, but if it's 32 degrees Fahrenheit you'll definitely need to wrap up!

32 DEGREES CELSIUS

Rhyme time

Remember these two rhymes and you can't go wrong:

Celsius	Fahrenheit
30 is hot,	*32's freezing,*
20 is nice,	*50 is not,*
10 is chilly,	*68's pleasant,*
0 is ice!	*85's hot!*

32 DEGREES FAHRENHEIT

CLOUDS

You'll have noticed that clouds come in many shapes and sizes, but did you know that different kinds of clouds have different names? Here are some of them:

How to remember

One way of identifying clouds is by looking at how high up they are. To help you with this, think of **CASE**:

Cirrus are the high clouds.
Alto clouds are at middle height.
Stratus are the low clouds.
Earth is where you're looking up from.

More ways to remember

These descriptions for common cloud types should also help you when it comes to recalling their names.

Cumulus are white, puffy clouds that look like cotton wool. So, to remember the world *cumulus*, think of *comfy cotton wool*.

Stratus are flat clouds, spread out straight across the sky. So ... *stratus = straight*.

Nimbus clouds are rain clouds, so the following phrase might help: *Run nimbly to avoid rain from nimbus clouds.*

COLOURS OF THE RAINBOW

Did you know that the bands of colour in a rainbow always appear in the same order? Red is always on the outside, followed by orange, then yellow, green, blue, indigo and violet. So, the next time you want to draw a rainbow, you can impress your friends by getting the order right – as long as you can remember it, that is.

How to remember

The initial letters of this phrase will help you to get those colours in the right order every time:

Richard Of York Gave Battle In Vain.

(Red, Orange, Yellow, Green, Blue, Indigo, Violet.)

In case you're wondering, 'Richard of York' probably refers to Richard III, who was King of England from 1483 until 1485. The battle he gave 'in vain' was the Battle of Bosworth Field during the Wars of the Roses, because he lost and had the unfortunate honour of becoming the last English king to die in combat.

PLANETS

Earth is one of nine planets in our solar system (if you include the dwarf planet Pluto). In order of distance from the Sun, starting with the closest, they are:

Mercury, **V**enus, **E**arth, **M**ars, **J**upiter, **S**aturn, **U**ranus, **N**eptune and **P**luto.

How to remember

Use this handy phrase to remember which order the planets come in:

My Very Eager Mother Just Served Us Nine Pizzas.

Or, if you want to leave out poor old Pluto, you could go with:

My Very Eager Mother Just Served Us Nachos.

Alternatively, you might want to be able to list the planets by size. From largest to smallest, they go:

Jupiter, **S**aturn, **U**ranus, **N**eptune, **E**arth, **V**enus, **M**ars, **M**ercury, **P**luto.

To remember them in that order, use this:

Julie Seriously Underestimated Nina's Eight Vicious Marshmallow-Munching Pandas.

STARS

There are so many stars in the sky that you could never hope to remember them all. However, you can learn the nine brightest stars that are visible from Earth at night. Here are their names, along with the constellations to which they belong:

Sirius, in Canis Major
Canopus, in Carina
Rigil Kent, in Centaurus
Arcturus, in Boötes
Vega, in Lyra
Capella, in Auriga
Rigel, in Orion
Procyon, in Canis Minor
Achernar, in Eridanus

How to remember

Take the first letters of each star to make this memorable phrase:

Stars **C**an **R**un **A**nd
Volley **C**risp **R**ed **P**erfect **A**pples.

> ### Did you know?
> Of all the stars listed here, Sirius (also known as the Dog Star) appears brightest. Its constellation, Canis Major, means 'Greater Dog' in Latin. Sirius is not actually brighter than the other stars, but it looks brighter from Earth because of how close it is to our solar system.

PHASES OF THE MOON

If you look up at the Moon every night, you'll notice that it seems to either grow (wax) or shrink (wane) as it travels round the Earth. However, the Moon doesn't really change shape or size – it just looks like it does. That's because a different part of it is visible each night.

At the beginning of the Moon's cycle, it appears as a very thin crescent. The Moon then seems to grow every night until it is a full circle in the sky, known as a Full Moon. These different stages are known as phases.

How to remember

When the Moon is waning, it looks a little like a letter 'C'. When it's full, it looks like an 'O'. When it's waxing, it's like a 'D'. So, if you keep in mind the word 'COD', it'll help you to remember the Moon's phases and recognize them in the night sky.

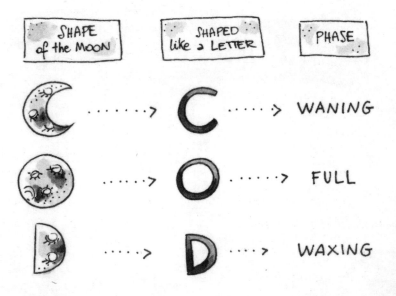

GENIUS GEOGRAPHY

Ways to remember your way around
a map ... or a geography lesson.

NORTH, EAST, SOUTH AND WEST

If you're looking at a map to find your way around, it's always useful
to understand map directions. If you think of directions as being like
a clock face, north is at 12 o'clock, east is at 3 o'clock, south is at 6
o'clock and west is at 9 o'clock.

How to remember

Here are five different
phrases will help you
to recall the order of
the directions around
that clock face. Pick
the one you find most
memorable and it
won't let you down.

1. *N*ever *E*at *S*oggy
   *W*affles.

2. *N*ever *E*at *S*hredded *W*heat.

3. *N*ever *E*at *S*limy *W*orms.

4. *N*ever *E*nter *S*anta's *W*orkshop.

5. *N*aughty *E*lephants
   *S*quirt *W*ater.

MAP READING

Maps are commonly divided up into boxes, which have smaller squares inside them. Each of the lines making up these boxes are numbered, with 'eastings' running from west to east and 'northings' running from south to north. Combining these numbers gives you a grid reference, so that you can find an exact spot on the map.

So, for example, if you have the grid reference '123456', '123' refers to numbers running across the map and '456' relates to numbers going up and down the map. Find these numbers, follow the lines, and the point at which the two lines meet is the place you're looking for.

How to remember

It's important to remember that the first number takes you across the map and the second number takes you up the map. This phrase should help you to do that:

Onwards and upwards!

LONGITUDE AND LATITUDE

Lines of longitude and latitude are the criss-crossing lines that you find on globes and maps of the world. The lines that go up and down, from the North Pole to the South Pole, are all the same length and are called lines of longitude.

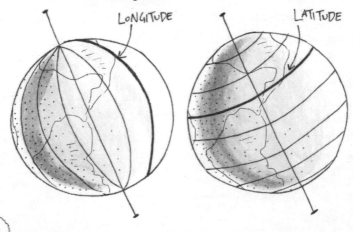

LONGITUDE   LATITUDE

The parallel lines that run around the Earth like hoops are called lines of latitude. Unlike the lines of longitude, lines of latitude vary in length. The line that goes around the middle of the Earth, known as the equator, is the longest line of latitude because this is where the Earth is at its fattest.

How to remember

To remember that the equally sized lines going up and down the Earth are the lines of longitude, just think:

*Lines of **long**itude are all as **long** as one another.*

For lines of latitude, focus on the middle line that goes around the Earth's fattest point.

Lat = fat

TROPICS OF CANCER AND CAPRICORN

The Tropics of Cancer and Capricorn are both lines of latitude, so they go around the Earth.

The Tropic of Cancer is located 23.5 degrees north of the equator. At noon, usually on 21st June each year, the Sun is directly over the line, making it the first day of summer in the northern hemisphere and the first day of winter in the southern hemisphere.

For the Tropic of Cancer, the reverse is true. It's 23.5 degrees south of the equator, and the Sun is directly over the line at noon around 21st December each year. This signals the first day of summer in the southern hemisphere and the first day of winter in the northern hemisphere.

How to remember

Notice the ***n*** in the middle of *Ca**n**cer* and the ***o*** in Capric**o**rn, and bear in mind these two reminders:

1. *Ca**n**cer is **n**orth of the equator.*
2. *Capric**o**rn is on the **o**ther side.*

CONTINENTS

The Earth is split up into seven large areas of land, called continents. The continents are: Africa, Antarctica, Asia, Australia, Europe, North America and South America.

How to remember

This phrase shares its initials with the seven continents of the world:

*E*at *A*n *A*pple *A*s *A N*ice *S*nack.

(*E*urope, *A*sia, *A*frica, *A*ustralia, *A*ntarctica, *N*orth America, *S*outh America.)

Or, you could try this one:

*A*ll *A*verage *A*nteaters *E*njoy *A*nts ... *N*ot *A*unts, I *S*aid *A*nts.

(*A*sia, *A*frica, *A*ntarctica, *E*urope, *A*ustralia ... *N*orth *A*merica, *S*outh *A*merica.)

Sing a song

If you would prefer a song to help you with the continents, try this one out. It's to be sung to the tune of 'Frère Jacques':

North America, South America,
(Frère Jacques, Frère Jacques,)

Australia, Australia,
(Dormez-vous? Dormez-vous?)

Don't forget Antarctica
(Sonnez les matines,)

Africa and Asia
(Sonnez les matines,)

And Europe, and Europe.
(Ding, dang, dong, ding, dang, dong.)

> **Did you know?**
> You might wonder why Antarctica (the South Pole) is
> considered a continent, but the Arctic (North Pole) is not. This
> is because Antarctica is a land mass like the other continents,
> whereas the Arctic is a sea covered in moving ice.

OCEANS

The five oceans of the world are the Antarctic, Arctic, Atlantic, Indian
and Pacific. The largest is the Pacific, which stretches between Asia
and the Americas, and covers around a third of the Earth's surface.
The Arctic, on the other hand, covers no more than 3 per cent of the
Earth's surface, making it the smallest ocean.

How to remember

You are an amazing person, and that's all you need to think of to
remember the names of the five oceans!

*I **A**m **A**n **A**mazing **P**erson.*
*(**I**ndian, **A**ntarctic, **A**rctic, **A**tlantic, **P**acific.)*

Remembering the oceans in size order from smallest to largest is a
little trickier, but this phrase should help:

***Arctic Ant**s **Ind**ulgently **At**e **Pa**sta.*
*(**Arctic**, **Ant**arctic, **In**dian, **Atl**antic, **Pa**cific.)*

THE GREAT LAKES

The Great Lakes are five huge lakes that are found close to the border between the United States of America and Canada. From west to east, their names are Lake Superior, Lake Michigan, Lake Huron, Lake Erie and Lake Ontario.

How to remember

To remember the names of the lakes in their west-to-east order, think:

Sam's **M**ighty **H**orse **E**ats **O**ats.
(**S**uperior, **M**ichigan, **H**uron, **E**rie, **O**ntario.)

If you don't need to know them in order, but just want to remember their names, an easier way is to just remember one word:

HOMES
(**H**uron, **O**ntario, **M**ichigan, **E**rie, **S**uperior)

> **Did you know?**
> Together, the five Great Lakes hold 21 per cent of all the fresh water on the surface of the Earth!

RIVERS

The three longest rivers in the world are estimated to be the Nile (in Africa), the Amazon (in South America) and the Yangtze (in Asia). Here's how long they are:

Nile	6,650 kilometres
Amazon	6,400 kilometres
Yangtze	6,300 kilometres

How to remember

Don't want to swim all the way along these rivers? Just say:

NAY
(**N**ile, **A**mazon, **Y**angtze)

MOUNTAINS

The three tallest mountains on Earth are all in Asia. They are:

Everest   8,849 metres
K2   8,611 metres
Kangchenjunga   8,586 metres

How to remember

Remember them in order by asking yourself this question:

***Ever K**ayaked to Timbuk**tu** with a **Kang**aroo?*
*(**Ever**est, **K2**, **Kang**chenjunga.)*

DESERTS

The three largest hot deserts in the world are the Sahara (in Africa), the Arabian and the Gobi (both in Asia). Here's how much land they each cover:

Sahara   8,600,000 square kilometres
Arabian 2,300,000 square kilometres
Gobi   1,300,000 square kilometres

How to remember

If you spend too much time in the heat of a desert, your energy levels might **SAG** (**S**ahara, **A**rabian, **G**obi).

CLIMATE

Planet Earth has five main climate zones: tropical, dry, temperate, cold (or continental) and polar.

The tropical zone is mainly around the equator, between the Tropics of Cancer and Capricorn (see page 75). Further out to the north and south are the dry zones. Head further out still and you reach the temperate zones, where the weather is milder. Beyond that are the colder continental zones. Finally, as you move towards the North and South Poles, you reach the polar zones.

Rhyme time

It's hot and humid in the tropics,
With dry zones either side.
Soon you'll find it's temperate,
Then cold will conquer mild.
When you reach the polar waste,
You'd better get inside with haste!

How to remember

To remember how the zones spread across the planet, imagine a person wrapped up in layers of jumpers, with a bare head and bare feet. They'd be hot in the middle but cold at the top and bottom, just like the Earth's climate!

VOLCANOES

The Earth's three most active volcanoes are Mount Etna (on the island of Sicily, Italy), Stromboli (an island off the coast of Sicily) and Yasur (on the island of Vanuatu in the South Pacific).

How to remember

Just think of the initial letters of this hard-to-forget phrase:

***M**um **E**ats **S**melly **Y**oghurt!*
*(**M**ount **E**tna, **S**tromboli, **Y**asur.)*

Did you know?
In the last 10,000 years, more than 1,500 volcanoes have erupted on land on Earth.

AMERICAN STATES

The United States of America is divided into 50 states. That's a lot to remember!

Rhyme time

This anonymous poem won't just help you to memorize all 50 states – it'll ensure you remember them in alphabetical order.

Alabama and Alaska, Arizona, Arkansas,
California, Colorado and Connecticut and more.
Delaware, Florida, Georgia, Hawaii and Idaho,
Illinois, Indiana, Iowa, still 35 to go.

Kansas and Kentucky, Louisiana, Maine,
Maryland, Massachusetts and good old Michigan,
Minnesota, Mississippi, Missouri and Montana,
Nebraska's 27, number 28's Nevada.

Next, New Hampshire and New Jersey,
And way down, New Mexico,
Then New York, North Carolina,
North Dakota, Ohio.

Oklahoma, Oregon, Pennsylvania, now let's see,
Rhode Island, South Carolina, South Dakota, Tennessee.
There's Texas, then there's Utah,
Vermont, I'm almost through,
Virginia, then there's Washington and West Virginia, too.
Could Wisconsin be the last one in the 49?
No, Wyoming is the last state in the 50 states that rhyme.

> ### Did you know?
> There are 50 stars on the USA flag.
> That's one for every state.

AMERICAN STATE CAPITALS

Here are some memory tricks for remembering the capital cities of all 50 American states.

How to remember

Being able to recall the capitals of 50 states might seem almost impossible, but if you break them down into groups and use their initials to form silly, memorable sentences, it becomes much easier. Here's how it's done:

Group One

State	Capital
Alabama	**M**ontgomery
Alaska	**J**uneau
Arizona	**P**hoenix
Arkansas	**L**ittle Rock
California	**S**acramento
Colorado	**D**enver
Connecticut	**H**artford
Delaware	**D**over
Florida	**T**allahassee
Georgia	**A**tlanta

My **J**umping **P**ony **L**ikes **S**houting '**D**elicious **H**ot **D**ogs!' **T**otally **A**mazing!

Group Two

State	Capital
Hawaii	**H**onolulu
Idaho	**B**oise
Illinois	**S**pringfield
Indiana	**I**ndianapolis
Iowa	**D**es Moines
Kansas	**T**opeka
Kentucky	**F**rankfort
Louisiana	**B**aton Rouge
Maine	**A**ugusta
Maryland	**A**nnapolis

How Big Should I Decide To Finally Build An Ark?

Group Three

State	Capital
Massachusetts	**B**oston
Michigan	**L**ansing
Minnesota	**S**aint Paul
Mississippi	**J**ackson
Missouri	**J**efferson City
Montana	**H**elena
Nebraska	**L**incoln
Nevada	**C**arson City
New Hampshire	**C**oncord
New Jersey	**T**renton

Beastly Lions Slurp Juicy Jellies Happily, Looking Completely Cool, Too!

Group Four

State	Capital
New Mexico	**S**anta Fe
New York	**A**lbany
North Carolina	**R**aleigh
North Dakota	**B**ismarck
Ohio	**C**olumbus
Oklahoma	**O**klahoma City
Oregon	**S**alem
Pennsylvania	**H**arrisburg
Rhode Island	**P**rovidence
South Carolina	**C**olumbia

***S**erious **A**nimals **R**ead **B**ooks '**C**os **O**ther **S**illy **H**oppy **P**enguins **C**an't.*

Group Five

State	Capital
South Dakota	**P**ierre
Tennessee	**N**ashville
Texas	**A**ustin
Utah	**S**alt Lake City
Vermont	**M**ontpelier
Virginia	**R**ichmond
Washington	**O**lympia
West Virginia	**C**harleston
Wisconsin	**M**adison
Wyoming	**C**heyenne

***P**aul's **N**ephew **A**ustin **S**pilt **M**ilk
Right **O**n **C**harlie's **M**um's **C**at!*

85

CENTRAL AMERICAN COUNTRIES

The group of seven countries found just to the south of the USA and Mexico are collectively known as Central America. They are Guatemala, Belize, El Salvador, Honduras, Nicaragua, Costa Rica and Panama.

How to remember

Keep in mind this silly sentence, which shares its initial letters with Mexico and the eight Central American countries:

My Great Big Elephant Has No Custard Pies.
(Mexico, Guatemala, Belize, El Salvador, Honduras, Nicaragua, Costa Rica, Panama.)

SOUTH AMERICAN CAPITALS

To the south of Central America lies South America. Starting in Guyana in the north and heading anti-clockwise around the continent, South America is made up of:

Country	Capital
Guyana	Georgetown
Venezuela	Caracas
Colombia	Bogotá
Ecuador	Quito
Peru	Lima
Bolivia	La Paz
Chile	Santiago
Argentina	Buenos Aires
Uruguay	Montevideo
Paraguay	Asunción
Brazil	Brasília
French Guiana	Cayenne
Suriname	Paramaribo

How to remember

A great way of remembering a list of things is to turn it into a story. This example takes the South American capitals and turns them into a tale about a very unusual road trip:

*One day, **George** (**George**town) got in his **car** (**Car**acas) and drove through a **bog** (**Bog**otá) without **quit**ting (**Quit**o). He put his pet **lemur** (**Lima**) on his **lap** (**La P**az); the one he got from **Sant**a (**Sant**iago). He wound down the window for some fresh **air** (Buenos **Air**es), then stopped to make a **video** (Monte**video**) of a man and **a son** (**Asun**ción). He then had a picnic of **Brazil** (**Bras**ília) nuts with **cayenne** (**Cayenne**) pepper. And that is where this **para**graph (**Para**maribo) ends.*

ISLANDS

The world's five biggest islands, in size order, are: Greenland, New Guinea, Borneo, Madagascar and Baffin.

How to remember

This sentence includes a reference to each of those islands:

*My **green new guinea** pig was **born** with **a scar** shaped like a pu**ffin**. (**Green**land, **New Guinea**, **Born**eo, Madag**ascar**, Ba**ffin**.)*

MEDITERRANEAN ISLANDS

The main islands in the Mediterranean Sea, from west (near Spain) to east (near Turkey) are: Balearic Islands, Sardinia, Corsica, Sicily, Crete and Cyprus.

How to remember

Keep this phrase in mind and you won't go wrong:

***Bal**loons in **sardin**es **cause silly crates** of **soup**.*
*(**Bal**earic Islands, **Sardin**ia, **Cors**ica, **Sicily**, **Crete**, **Cyp**rus.)*

STALACTITES AND STALAGMITES

Stalactites and stalagmites are the long, spiky, limestone rock formations found in caves. They are created from drips of water that fall from the roof of the cave and land on the ground. The stalactites are the stone spikes that come down from the ceiling and the stalagmites are the ones that rise up from the ground – but how do you remember the difference?

STALACTITE

STALAGMITE

How to remember

Here are three memory tricks you could use for telling stalactites from stalagmites:

1. *Stala**c**tites **c**ome down from the **c**eiling, Stala**g**mites **g**row up from the **g**round.*

2. *Stalac**tite**s stick **tight** to the ceiling. Stalag**mites might** one day reach up and touch them.*

3. Imagine the 'mites' as tiny creatures climbing up someone's legs. *The **mites** go up, the **tites** come down!*

GEOLOGY

Geology is the study of the Earth's structure and origins. Earth has been around for several billion years, so geologists divide its past into different periods. Some of these periods, such as the Jurassic and Cretaceous, are famously associated with dinosaurs. Others are less well known.

These are the 11 main geological periods, ranging from the Cambrian (when plant and animal life began to develop) to the Quaternary (which you're living in at the moment!):

Cambrian:	541–485 million years ago
Ordovician:	485–444 million years ago
Silurian:	444–419 million years ago
Devonian:	419–359 million years ago
Carboniferous:	359–299 million years ago
Permian:	299–252 million years ago
Triassic:	252–201 million years ago
Jurassic:	201–145 million years ago
Cretaceous:	145–66 million years ago
Tertiary:	66–2.6 million years ago
Quaternary:	2.6 million years ago to the present

How to remember

The initial letters of this phrase will help take you back in time!

Can Ordinary Students Date Carbon Perfectly, Then Join Courses? Tough Question!
(Cambrian, Ordovician, Silurian, Devonian, Carboniferous, Permian, Triassic, Jurassic, Cretaceous, Tertiary, Quaternary.)

LIFE ON EARTH

Ways to remember the wonders of nature.

CHARACTERISTICS OF LIFE

How do you know if something is alive? All living things, including plants, bugs, animals and, of course, you, share these seven characteristics:

1. **M**ovement – even plants have roots that move and their leaves move towards the Sun.

2. **R**espiration – the process where living organisms release energy (when you breathe, for example).

3. **S**ensitivity – every living thing can sense things that affect them.

4. **G**rowth – if something is alive, then at some point it will grow.

5. **R**eproduction – every living species has the ability to create more of itself. If it didn't, it wouldn't be around for long!

6. **E**xcretion – every living thing needs to dispose of waste products. As a human, you do this by going to the toilet.

7. **N**utrition – all living things need it. Plants get energy by photosynthesis (see page 93), and animals acquire it from eating and drinking.

How to remember

Take a look at the bold initial letters of each of the words on that list and remember whose name they spell: **MRS GREN**.

PARTS OF A PLANT

Plants have different parts that help them to survive. All plants have a stem to enable them to grow. A plant's roots absorb water and nutrients from the soil. The stem allows the plant to move water and nutrients from its roots to its leaves. The leaves have the job of capturing energy from the Sun.

How to remember

To keep the **s**tem, **l**eaves and **r**oots in mind, think of ...

***S**tarving **L**ions **R**oar!*

PARTS OF A FLOWER

Flowers have a number of different parts. The sepals are the leaf-like elements around the outside of the flower. The stamen is the male part which makes pollen. The carpel is the female part, and collects the pollen. The petals are brightly coloured to attract insects.

How to remember

Keep this sentence in mind:

***Se**e your **pet sta**nding on the **carpe**t.*
*(**Se**pal, **pet**al, **sta**men, **carpe**l.)*

TREES

The two main types of tree are deciduous and coniferous. Deciduous trees are the ones that lose their leaves in autumn. Coniferous trees keep their leaves all year round.

How to remember

For **decid**uous trees, think of:

*I **decide** to leave in the autumn.*

For **conifer**ous trees, try using this:

*It would be a big **con if fir**s shed their leaves, because they're supposed to be evergreen.*

PLANT GROWTH

Plants need four things to grow: sunlight, water, air and nutrients.

How to remember

Just think of a **SWAN** made of plants! (**S**unlight, **W**ater, **A**ir, **N**utrients.)

PHOTOSYNTHESIS

Photosynthesis is a process through which green leaves turn sunlight, water and carbon dioxide into sugar that helps the plant to grow. During this process, oxygen is also produced and released back into the air as a waste product.

Rhyme time

The ins and outs of photosynthesis can be tricky to get to grips with – but not if you have a rhyme to remember!

The plant takes carbon dioxide and water,
And then the Sun shines, just like it oughta.
This turns them to sugar, the plant's favourite food,
And oxygen too, which it kicks out ... how rude!

WHAT ANIMALS EAT

All animals can be separated into three different groups, based on what they eat.

• Herbivores are plant-eaters.

• Carnivores are meat-eaters.

• Omnivores eat both plants and meat.

How to remember

• Herbivores: a **herb** is a plant, so an animal that eats those is a **herb**ivore.

• Carnivores: remember that chilli con **carn**e has meat in it. So **carn**ivore means meat-eater.

• Omnivores: an animal that eats both meat and plants could eat a ham-and-spinach **om**elette, as it's an **om**nivore.

VERTEBRATES AND INVERTEBRATES

All animals are either vertebrates or invertebrates.

Vertebrates are animals with a backbone or spine. Birds, fish, amphibians, reptiles and mammals are all vertebrates.

Invertebrates are animals that have no backbone. Insects, octopuses, crabs and coral are all examples of invertebrates.

How to remember

To remember the groups of animals that are vertebrates, just think:

*Vertebrates must **B**e kept on a **FARM**.*
*(**B**irds, **F**ish, **A**mphibians, **R**eptiles, **M**ammals.)*

Any animal that isn't in one of these categories is an ***in**vertebrate*. It doesn't fit ***in***.

BIG CATS

There are many kinds of wild cat, but four in particular are known as the big cats. Not only are they big, but they're also the only cats that can roar! The four big cats are leopards, lions, tigers and jaguars.

How to remember

Remember the four big cats with this sentence:

***Leo* li**kes **t**o **j**ump.*
*(**Leo**pard, **li**on, **t**iger, **j**aguar.)*

Did you know?
Big cats might be able to let out an
impressive roar, but they can't purr!

MARSUPIALS

Marsupials are mammals who give birth to underdeveloped young. Because of this, many female marsupials have a pouch for their babies to stay safe in. Most marsupial species live in Australia. However, marsupials are also found in North, Central and South America.

How to remember

The best-known marsupials are wallabies, kangaroos, wombats and koalas. These marsupials often sleep during the day, so you can think of them by shouting:

WaKey WaKey!
(Wallabies, Kangaroos, Wombats, Koalas.)

CAMELS

Have you ever noticed that some camels have one hump and others have two? That's because there are two types of camel. The dromedary has one hump, while the Bactrian has two.

How to remember

Dromedary starts with a 'd', and an upper-case 'D' lying on its side looks like one hump. Bactrian starts with a 'B' – turn that 'B' on its side and your have two humps.

ELEPHANTS

You probably already know that there are African elephants and Indian elephants – but can you tell the difference between them? The easiest way is by size. African elephants are larger than Indian elephants, and they also have bigger ears.

How to remember

Simply think of it this way: Africa is larger than India, and African elephants are bigger than Indian elephants.

INSECTS

Five of the most common groups of insect are: bees, beetles, butterflies, flies and grasshoppers.

How to remember

Remember the insect world's big five with this phrase:

Two **bees** and two **flies** hopped on the **grass**.
(**Bee**s, **bee**tles, butter**flies**, **flies**, **grass**hoppers.)

> **Did you know?**
> It is estimated that insects make up 90 per cent of all animal species on Earth.

DAYS GONE BY

Ways to remember some highs
(and lows) of human history.

BCE OR CE?

When learning about the past, you'll often see that old dates include
either 'CE' or 'BCE'. The abbreviation 'CE' stands for 'Common Era',
while 'BCE' stands for 'Before Common Era'. Common Era is the period
of time that begins with the traditional date of Jesus Christ's birth – in
other words, the Christian era. Before Common Era is everything that
came before this.

How to remember

B comes before **C** in the alphabet, so **B**CE comes before **C**E.

BC OR AD?

You may sometimes see 'BC' used instead of 'BCE', and 'AD' used
instead of 'CE'. 'BC' stands for 'Before Christ', while 'AD' means
Anno Domini – a Latin phrase meaning 'Year of our Lord'. These
abbreviations have historically been used by Chirstians to divide the
time before and after when they believe that Jesus was born.

How to remember

BC comes **b**efore, **A**D follows **a**fter.

DINOSAUR DAYS

The Triassic, Jurassic and Cretaceous are the names of the three geological periods when dinosaurs roamed the Earth. But what happened when?

Triassic Period (252–201 million years ago)
This is when the first dinosaurs and pterosaurs (small flying reptiles) lived.

Jurassic Period (201–145 million years ago)
This is when bigger dinosaurs such as diplodocus, stegosaurus and brachiosaurus lived.

Cretaceous Period (145–66 million years ago)
This is when Tyrannosaurus rex and triceratops lived. Close to the end of this period, dinosaurs became extinct.

How to remember

Try using these phrases to help:

*In the **Tri**assic, a **tri**ckle of dinosaurs appeared.*

*The **J**urassic **p**eriod was **j**am-**p**acked with large dinosaurs.*

*In the **Cre**taceous period, **cre**atures thrive,
But by the end, no dinos survive!*

And, to remember the order the periods come in, you could:

***Try ju**ggling **cre**am cakes!*
*(**Tri**assic, **Ju**rassic, **Cre**taceous.)*

PREHISTORIC AGES

The earliest humans lived through three prehistoric ages, which are known as the Stone Age, the Bronze Age and the Iron Age.

How to remember

Keep this phrase in mind:

***S**tacey **A**lways **B**eats **A**rnie **I**n **A**thletics.*
*(**S**tone **A**ge, **B**ronze **A**ge, **I**ron **A**ge.)*

STONE AGE ERAS

The Stone Age was when humans first began to use tools made of stone. The Stone Age is divided into three eras: the Palaeolithic, the Mesolithic and the Neolithic.

How to remember

Just think of a Stone Age family of ***P**a, **M**a* and their ***Ne**w baby.*
*(**Pa**laeolithic, **M**esolithic, **Ne**olithic.)*

ANCIENT CIVILIZATIONS

The Egyptians, Greeks and Romans all built famous ancient civilizations. Can you remember that the Egyptians came first, then the Greeks and then the Romans?

How to remember

The initial letters of this phrase should make it easy:

Ahmed Eats Apples, Grapes And Raspberries.
(*Ancient Egyptians, Ancient Greeks, Ancient Romans.*)

An even easier way is to simply remember that they arrived in alphabetical order.

GREEK PHILOSOPHERS

The great thinkers of ancient Greece were called philosophers. The most famous ones were known as Socrates, Plato and Aristotle.

How to remember

Just think of **SPA**.
(**S**ocrates, **P**lato, **A**ristotle)

Alternatively, remember how they were all:

So PopulAr.
(**So**crates, **P**lato, **A**ristotle.)

SEVEN WONDERS OF THE WORLD

The Seven Wonders of the World were listed by the ancient Greeks as the best sights to visit around the Mediterranean. They are:

1. The Mausoleum of Halicarnassus

2. The Temple of Artemis at Ephesus

3. The Lighthouse of Alexandria

4. The Hanging Gardens of Babylon

5. The Colossus of Rhodes

6. The Statue of Zeus at Olympia

7. The Pyramids of Giza

How to remember

A great way of remembering lists is to make up a story in your head. To remember the Seven Wonders, try coming up with a story where you travel round visiting each one. The example below is one of many ways in which it could work, but if you come up with your own story you'll remember it even better.

On Monday I meandered through the Mausoleum of Halicarnassus.

On Tuesday I took in the Temple of Artemis at Ephesus before tea.

Wednesday's wonder was the Lighthouse of Alexandria.

On Thursday I hung out in the Hanging Gardens of Babylon.

Friday finished with the famous Colossus of Rhodes.

On Saturday I saw the Statue of Zeus at Olympia.

On Sunday I sailed up the River Nile to see the Pyramids of Giza.

> **Did you know?**
> The Pyramids of Giza is the only one of the Seven Wonders still around today.

ROMAN EMPERORS

The best-known Roman leader was the general and statesman Julius Caesar, but the five Roman emperors who came after him are trickier to remember. They were Augustus, Tiberius, Caligula, Claudius and Nero.

How to remember

Use this phrase to help you with the first letters of each of their names:

Another **T**om **C**at **C**aught **N**apping.
(**A**ugustus, **T**iberius, **C**aligula, **C**laudius, **N**ero.)

ROMAN NUMERALS

In ancient Rome, numbers were written as letters. Only the numbers one, five, ten, 50, 100, 500 and 1,000 were given letters of their own. Other numbers were all made up from combinations of those letters. Here are the letters they used:

One	I
Five	V
Ten	X
50	L
100	C
500	D
1,000	M

How to remember

Try using this phrase to help you to remember the letters and the order they come in:

I Value **X**-rays – **L**ucy **C**an't **D**rink **M**ilk.

INVENTORS

Everything you use today has been either invented or discovered at some point. Here are five famous inventors and tricks to remember their life-changing innnovations.

Alexander Graham Bell

Bell invented the first telephone in 1876. To remember his name, just think of a telephone ringing like a **bell**.

Thomas Edison

Edison invented a bulb that burned brightly for a few hours, leading to the lighting systems we use today. In 1882, he formed the Edison Electric Illuminating Company of New York and electric lighting was introduced to parts of Manhattan. To remember him, imagine a man named **Eddie** with his **son** ('Eddie's son' sounds like Edison) and a big light bulb above their heads.

John Logie Baird

In 1926, Baird (pronounced '**bear**-d') demonstrated the televising of moving objects – he had invented the TV! To remember him, just think of a **bear** dancing around on a television screen.

The Wright Brothers

The first powered air flight was made by brothers Wilbur and Orville Wright in 1903. Use this phrase to remember them: *The first plane flew **(W)right** up into the air!*

Alexander Fleming

Fleming discovered the antibiotic penicillin by accident in 1928, when some mould grew on a Petri dish he had left uncovered. Penicillin would go on to save millions of lives. To remember Fleming's discovery, use this phrase: *Fleming didn't make a **pen**ny from **pen**icillin.*

ENGLISH KINGS AND QUEENS

England has had lots of kings and queens over the years. As you'll see from the list below, it's a lot to try to remember:

William I 'The Conqueror' (1066–87)

William II 'Rufus' (1087–1100)

Henry I (1100–35)

Stephen (1135–54)

Henry II (1154–89)

Richard I 'The Lionheart' (1189–99)

John (1199–1216)

Henry III (1216–72)

Edward I (1272–1307)

Edward II (1307–27)

Edward III (1327–77)

Richard II (1377–99)

Henry IV (1399–1413)

Henry V (1413–22)

Henry VI (1422–61 and 1470–71)

Edward IV (1461–70 and 1471–83)

Edward V (1483)

Richard III (1483–85)

Henry VII (1485–1509)

Henry VIII (1509–47)

Edward VI (1547–53)

Lady Jane Grey (1553–53)

Mary I (1553–58)

Elizabeth I (1558–1603)

James I (and VI of Scotland) (1603–25)

Charles I (1625– 49)

Charles II (1660–85)

James II (and VII of Scotland) (1685–88)

William III (1689–1702) and Mary II (1689–94)

Anne (1702–14)

George I (1714–27)

George II (1727–60)

George III (1760–1820)

George IV (1820–30)

William IV (1830–37)

Victoria (1837–1901)

Edward VII (1901–10)

George V (1910–36)

Edward VIII (1936)

George VI (1936–52)

Elizabeth II (1952–present)

Rhyme time

Fortunately, there's an excellent rhyme to help you with that huge list of kings and queens. This one has been around for many years, and takes you right up to the present day:

Willie, Willie, Harry, Stee,
Harry, Dick, John, Harry Three,
One, Two, Three Eds, Richard Two,
Harrys Four, Five, Six ... then who?

Edwards Four, Five, Dick the Bad,
Harry twice, Ed Six the lad,
Mary, Bessie, James you ken,
Charlie, Charlie, James again,

Will and Mary, Anne of Gloria,
George times four, Will Four, Victoria,
Edward Seven next, and then,
Came George the Fifth in 1910.

Ned the Eighth soon abdicated,
So George Six was 'coronated',
Then number two Elizabeth,
And that's all folks ... until her death!

Did you know?

'Harry' is a common nickname for people called Henry – hence its use in the rhyme. The same goes for 'Bessie', which is a nickname for Queen Elizabeth I.

'James you ken', in the second verse, means 'James you know' in Scots – a reference to the fact that James I was also James VI of Scotland.

HENRY VIII'S WIVES

Henry VIII was King of England from 1509 to 1547. During his life he had six wives, whose names were Catherine of Aragon, Anne Boleyn, Jane Seymour, Anne of Cleves, Catherine Howard and Catherine Parr.

Rhyme time

This rhyme should help you with the order Henry's wives came in:

Kate 'n' Anne 'n' Jane,
'n' Anne 'n' Kate again 'n' again!

There's also a slightly gruesome rhyme you can use to remember how each of the wives ended up!

Divorced, beheaded, died,
Divorced, beheaded, survived.

ENGLISH ROYAL HOUSES

The main royal families (known as 'Royal Houses') to have ruled over England during the last one thousand years are:

Norman	(1066–1135)
Plantagenet	(1154–1399)
Lancaster	(1399–1461 and 1470–71)
York	(1461–70 and 1471–85)
Tudor	(1485–1603)
Stuart	(1603–49 and 1660–1714)
Hanover	(1714–1901)
Saxe-Coburg-Gotha	(1901–1917)
Windsor	(1917–present)

How to remember

Use the initial letters of this phrase to help you to remember those families in order:

No **P**lan **L**ike **Y**ours **T**o **S**tudy **H**istory **S**eriously **W**isely.
(**N**orman, **P**lantagenet, **L**ancaster, **Y**ork, **T**udor, **S**tuart, **H**anover, **S**axe-Coburg-Gotha, **W**indsor.)

THE GUNPOWDER PLOT

In the UK, 5th November is Bonfire Night. This marks the date in 1605 when a plot by Guy Fawkes and others to blow up the Houses of Parliament was foiled.

Rhyme time

This rhyme makes the date of Bonfire Night very difficult to forget:

Remember, remember, the fifth of November,
Gunpowder, treason and plot.
We know of no reason, why gunpowder treason,
Should ever be forgot.

THE PILGRIM FATHERS

The Pilgrim Fathers were the first American colonists, who sailed to North America on a ship called the *Mayflower* in 1620.

Rhyme time

Think of the 24-hour clock, where 16:20 (like the year 1620) would be 4.20 pm.

It's twenty past four,
Let's go ashore!

AMERICAN PRESIDENTS

There have been over 40 presidents of the USA. Four of them (Washington, Jefferson, Roosevelt (Theodore) and Lincoln) have their heads sculpted into Mount Rushmore. The full list of presidents is:

George Washington (1789–97)
John Adams (1797–1801)
Thomas Jefferson (1801–09)
James Madison (1809–17)
James Monroe (1817–25)
John Quincy Adams (1825–29)
Andrew Jackson (1829–37)
Martin Van Buren (1837–41)
William Henry Harrison (1841)
John Tyler (1841–45)
James K. Polk (1845–49)
Zachary Taylor (1849–50)
Millard Fillmore (1850–53)
Franklin Pierce (1853–57)
James Buchanan (1857–61)
Abraham Lincoln (1861–65)
Andrew Johnson (1865–69)
Ulysses S. Grant (1869–77)
Rutherford B. Hayes (1877–81)
James A. Garfield (1881)
Chester A. Arthur (1881–85)
Grover Cleveland (1885–89)
Benjamin Harrison (1889–93)

Grover Cleveland (1893–97)
William McKinley (1897–1901)
Theodore Roosevelt (1901–09)
William H. Taft (1909–13)
Woodrow Wilson (1913–21)
Warren G. Harding (1921–23)
Calvin Coolidge (1923–29)
Herbert Hoover (1929–33)
Franklin D. Roosevelt (1933–45)
Harry S. Truman (1945–53)
Dwight D. Eisenhower (1953–61)
John F. Kennedy (1961–63)
Lyndon B. Johnson (1963–69)
Richard M. Nixon (1969–74)
Gerald R. Ford (1974–77)
Jimmy Carter (1977–81)
Ronald Reagan (1981–89)
George Bush (1989–93)
Bill Clinton (1993–2001)
George W. Bush (2001–09)
Barack Obama (2009–17)
Donald J. Trump (2017–21)
Joseph R. Biden (2021–present)

Rhyme time

This clever poem lists all of the American presidents in order. It was written by an unknown poet, and some lines have been added over the years to keep it up-to-date.

George Washington leads them, the great and the true,
John Adams succeeds him and Jefferson too,
Madison follows and fifth comes Monroe,
With John Quincy Adams and Jackson below.

The term of Van Buren to Harrison's leads,
Tyler, Polk, Taylor, then Fillmore succeeds,
Pierce and Buchanan, and Lincoln in turn,
Is followed by Johnson and Grant, we discern.

Hayes, Garfield and Arthur, and Cleveland we score,
Then Harrison is followed by Cleveland once more,
Then comes McKinley and the full dinner pail,
And one called 'Teddy' who to Cuba did sail.

William Taft his government began,
And Woodrow Wilson, a marvellous man;
Harding and Coolidge are next in the rhyme,
Then Hoover and the people had a very hard time.

FDR was great in both peace and war,
Truman was striving for what we were fighting for,
The former General Eisenhower,
Brought the Republicans back to power.

John Kennedy's victory in the race,
Was for the New Frontier in the Age of Space,
Lyndon Johnson led the people, the free and the brave,
With a goal to achieve and a country to save.

The poem is so long that it continues on the next page!

Nixon swore to uphold our creed,
Of liberty, life and every man's need,
But by Nixon these rules were ignored,
So to take his place was President Ford.

Then came Carter with a cheery smile,
To run our country 'Southern Style',
Then Carter's smile left his face,
And Reagan came to take his place.

'Dutch' stayed two terms, Bush filled his station,
Bringing with him a 'kinder, gentler nation',
Clinton took over and served for eight years,
George W. followed, with Texan cheers.

The first African American was next in line,
Barack Obama in 2009,
Then along came celebrity Donald J. Trump,
Until Biden came in and Trump got the hump.

THE MOON LANDING

"That's one small step for a man,
One giant leap for mankind."

Those were Neil Armstrong's famous words when he became the first person to set foot on the Moon on 20th July 1969. Most people remember Neil Armstrong's name, but there were two other crew members aboard the mission. One was Buzz Aldrin, who followed Armstrong onto the Moon's surface. The other was Michael Collins, who had to stay behind on the Apollo 11 spacecraft to operate the controls.

How to remember
Remembering the names **A**rmstrong, **B**uzz and **C**ollins is as easy as **A, B, C**!

To remember the name of their spacecraft, replace the double 'l' in Apollo with a double '1': *Apo11o 11*.

DATES TO REMEMBER

History is packed with important dates. Even the best historians can't recall every single one, but there are memory techniques you can use to remember the ones you find most significant or interesting.

Rhyme time

If you make up rhymes around the dates you want to keep in mind, you should find they come back to you much more easily. Here are some examples, but you could try creating your own:

In 1912, in April,
The ship Titanic *was in peril.*

From 1914 for over four years,
World War I brought tears.

In the year 1917,
Russia's Revolution was seen.

From '39 to '45,
World War II came alive.

In space in 1969,
Neil Armstrong's Moon landing was fine.

SPECTACULAR SCIENCE

Ways to remember the secrets of science.

BRILLIANT MINDS

There have been many amazing scientists who have come up with incredible discoveries. Here are some of the most famous:

Archimedes

Archimedes was one of the great thinkers of ancient Greece. He came up with Archimedes' principle, which states that the buoyant force of an object equals the weight of the fluid it displaces. According to legend, he was struck by this thought while sitting in the bath. He was so happy that he ran through the streets naked, shouting "Eureka!"

Nicolaus Copernicus

Copernicus is the astronomer credited with first stating that the Earth travels around the Sun. This was big news at a time when most people believed Earth was the centre of the universe.

Galileo Galilei

This Italian scientist discovered that objects of the same material, but different weights, will fall at the same speed. The story goes that he demonstrated this by climbing to the top of the Leaning Tower of Pisa and dropping two balls of different weights. The balls hit the ground at the same time and Galileo was proven right. No one knows for sure if the Pisa experiment really happened, but it's a great story!

Sir Isaac Newton

Newton is often credited with discovering gravity. He supposedly came up with his theory of gravity after being struck on the head by an apple falling from a tree.

Henry Cavendish

This British scientist was the discoverer of 'inflammable air' – now known as hydrogen.

Charles Darwin

Darwin's many years of exploring the world led to him writing *On the Origin of Species*, in which he shared his theory of evolution.

Albert Einstein

One of the most famous scientists of more recent years, Einstein is best known for his theory of relativity. This theory states that an object's energy can be calculated by multiplying its mass by the speed of light squared. This is written as $E = mc^2$ (where 'E' is energy, 'm' is mass and 'c' is the speed of light).

Rhyme time

Here's a poem you can learn that will help you to remember all of these great scientists and their famous works:

The Greek Archimedes was a knowledge seeker,
Thought up his principle and yelled, "Eureka!"
Copernicus told us Earth circles the Sun,
While Galileo's weights both fell as one.
Newton's law of gravity was more than a wish,
And hydrogen was discovered by Mr Cavendish.
Darwin talked of evolution when no one else dared,
And Einstein taught us that $E = mc^2$.

ATOMS

Everything in the whole universe (even you!) is made of atoms. But what are atoms made from? Each atom contains protons (which have a positive electrical charge), electrons (negatively charged) and neutrons (neutral). The number of protons and electrons in an atom is always the same, meaning that all atoms are neutral.

How to remember

To know what makes up an atom, you just need to remember one word:

PEN
(**P**rotons, **E**lectrons, **N**eutrons)

WATER

When atoms bond together, they make a more complex structure called a molecule. One water molecule is made of two atoms of hydrogen (H) and one atom of oxygen (O). This is why water is known as H_2O.

How to remember

Picture this image and you'll find H_2O hard to forget:

Harry found **2 O**ctopuses
in the water.
(**H₂O**)

METALS

Metals are all around us in many shapes and forms. Different types of metal include iron, copper, lead, gold and silver. Most metals share these qualities:

- Strength

- High melting point

- Shiny appearance

- Solid at room temperature

- Malleable (able to be beaten into different shapes without breaking)

- Good conductor of electricity and heat

Rhyme time

Here's a verse that will help you to remember the six properties of metals:

They're shiny, strong and solid,
They conduct and they are malleable,
They do not melt easily,
That's why they are so valuable!

MAGNETS

If an object is magnetic, it will attract anything made of iron. You may have noticed that if you hold two magnets together they can either attract each other or push each other apart. This is because every magnet has two ends: a north pole and a south pole. The rule is that the opposite poles attract and the same poles repel.

How to remember

There is a common saying that 'opposites attract'. Just keep that in mind and you'll remember what happens when two magnets come together.

FOSSIL FUELS

Coal, oil and gas are known as fossil fuels. This is because they have formed over millions of years from the remains of prehistoric plants and animals.

If you need a reminder of what the three main fossil fuels are, use another word:

COG
(**C**oal, **O**il, **G**as)

Historically, people have used gas for tasks such as cooking, oil for powering engines and coal for heating. However, most of the energy people use every day comes from electricity, which can also come from fossil fuels indirectly. There are four steps to this process:

1. The fuel is burned to heat water and make steam.

2. The steam turns a turbine.

3. The turbine turns a generator.

4. The generator creates electricity.

How to remember
To remember the four-step process, you just need one word:

STaGE
(**S**team, **T**urbine, **a** **G**enerator, **E**lectricity)

RENEWABLE ENERGY

One big problem with fossil fuels is that once they have been used up, they can't be used again. That's why renewable energy sources provide a valuable alternative. Renewable energy can be generated over and over, without running out.

Examples of renewable energy sources include wind farms, wave power stations, biofuel power stations (where solid waste is burned), geothermal energy (which uses heat from inside the Earth), hydroelectric energy (which is produced by channelling water through tunnels) and solar energy from the Sun.

How to remember

This phrase can be used to remind you of six common renewable energy sources:

Why Waste Brilliantly Good Heat Sources?
(Wind, Wave, Biofuels, Geothermal, Hydroelectric, Solar.)

POTENTIAL AND KINETIC ENERGY

Potential, or stored energy, is energy waiting to happen. If you stand at the top of a hill while wearing roller-skates, you have potential energy.

Kinetic energy is movement energy. If you start skating down the hill, you have kinetic energy because you're moving.

How to remember

The letters in this phrase should remind you which type of energy is which:

It's potential when it's on pause, and kinetic when it's in motion.

THE ELECTROMAGNETIC SPECTRUM

Electromagnetic radiation consists of waves of charged particles travelling from one place to another. The waves vary in length, from short to long, in what is known as the electromagnetic spectrum.

Visible light is the only type of electromagnetic wave that your eyes can see, and its waves are split into the colours of the rainbow. Red waves are the longest and violet waves are the shortest.

The full spectrum, from the longest wave to the shortest, comprises:

- Radio waves

- Microwaves

- Infrared

- Visible light (red, orange, yellow, green, blue, indigo, violet)

- Ultraviolet

- X-rays

- Gamma rays

How to remember

There's a lot to remember there, but this phrase should make the full spectrum easier to bring to mind:

Rigorous **M**edics **I**nvestigate **V**ampires' **L**egs **U**sing **X**-ray **G**lasses. (**R**adio waves, **M**icrowaves, **I**nfrared, **V**isible **L**ight, **U**ltraviolet, **X**-rays, **G**amma rays.)

CHEMICAL COMPOUNDS

Chemical compounds are made from at least two chemical elements. Water, or H_2O, is an example of a compound (see page 114). Compounds are commonly grouped into the following categories:

- Acids – for example, citric acid found in lemons. Acids react with other chemicals.

- Bases – the opposite of an acid. These are measured on the pH scale. If a compound has a pH above seven, it is a base. If the pH is below seven, it is an acid.

- Salts – sometimes, bases and acids react to make a salt. One type of salt you'll already be familiar with is sodium chloride. That's the salt you sprinkle on your food!

- Oxides – these are compounds of elements with oxygen. One example of an oxide is iron oxide, better known as rust. Rust forms when iron forms a compound with oxygen.

- Organic – an organic compound contains carbon. Many carbohydrates, which are naturally found in some foods, are organic compounds.

How to remember

Try memorizing this sentence, which uses the initial letters of each of the above categories:

***A Base**ball **Sa**ved the **Ox**'s **Organ**s.*
*(**A**cids, **Base**s, **Sa**lts, **Ox**ides, **Organ**ic.)*

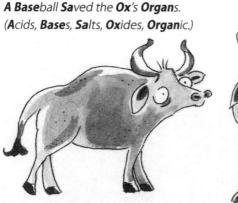

BIOLOGICAL CLASSIFICATIONS

There are seven basic categories in the animal and plant world. They follow each other in a particular order, with each category falling within the category above it.

The seven categories are:

- Kingdom
- Phylum
- Class
- Order
- Family
- Genus
- Species

A domestic cat, for example, would fall into the kingdom Animalia (because it's an animal), the phylum Chordata (meaning it has a backbone), the class Mammalia (because it's a mammal), the order Carnivora (because it eats meat), the family Felidae (a category covering all kinds of cat), the genus *Felis* (because it's a small cat) and the species *catus* (because it's of the domestic variety).

How to remember

Just remember that:

***K**ind **P**eople **C**an **O**ccasionally **F**eel **G**rumpy **S**uddenly.
(**K**ingdom, **P**hylum, **C**lass, **O**rder, **F**amily, **G**enus, **S**pecies.)*

THE HUMAN BODY

Ways to remember the most important
thing of all – your own body.

TEETH

Human teeth come in several different shapes and sizes. The four
types of adult teeth are:

- Incisors – the teeth at the front that help you to bite into food

- Canines – the pointed ones, for tearing food

- Premolars – these come behind the canines and can cut and grind

- Molars – these are at the back and are used just for grinding food

How to remember

Use this phrase to help you remember which tooth is which:

*My teeth bite **in**to
a **can** of **pre**tty
sweet **mola**sses.
(**In**cisors, **can**ines,
premolars, **mola**rs.)*

BLOOD

Blood is pumped around your body by your heart. Your blood travels by passing through little pipe-like vessels called arteries, capillaries and veins. Here's the difference between the three vessels:

- Arteries carry blood full of oxygen out of the heart.

- Capillaries are very thin vessels that allow blood to release oxygen through their walls and into the body's tissue.

- Veins take the blood back to the heart, where it can be refilled with oxygen.

How to remember

Think of the vessels' jobs like this:

Arteries send blood **a**way from the heart.
Capillaries let oxygen es**cap**e through their walls.
Veins re**ve**rse the blood's direction.

SENSES

Your senses are the tools you have for taking in information about the world around you. The five basic human senses are sight, smell, taste, hearing and touch.

How to remember

Just think of the five things you have on your face. You have eyes for sight, a nose to smell, a mouth to taste, ears to hear and skin for touch.

EYES

Eyes are very complex and are made up of lots of different parts to allow you to see. The main parts of the eye are:

- Sclera – the white part

- Iris – the coloured part

- Cornea – a clear dome that covers the iris and helps the eye to focus

- Pupil – the central black spot, which expands and contracts to allow light in

- Lens – helps to focus light on the retina

- Retina – transforms light into signals that the brain can pick up

- Optic nerve – carries signals from the retina to the brain

How to remember

This silly sentence and image should be a big help with remembering all those different parts:

SICk **P**enguins **L**ove i**RON**ing!
(**S**clera, **I**ris, **C**ornea, **P**upil, **L**ens, **R**etina, **O**ptic **N**erve.)

ORGANS

Organs are specialized parts of the body that each have their own vital job.

Rhyme time

This poem explains the jobs of some of the human body's key organs:

*Start with the **heart**, which pumps blood around inside,*
***Lungs** take in oxygen and expel carbon dioxide.*
*The **liver** cares for the blood, removing the bad stuff,*
*The **stomach** digests your food, even when it's tough.*
*The **intestines** absorb food and get rid of the waste,*
*Then the **bladder** stores urine, so you don't pee in haste!*

Did you know?
Skin is also considered an organ and is actually the largest organ of the human body.

MAGNIFICENT MATHS

Ways to remember how to do your sums.

THREE TIMES TABLE

If you ever find yourself stuck with your three times table, there's a quick cheat for working it out. To multiply any number by three, multiply it by two first and then add the original number to the total.

So, for 7 x 3, work out 7 x 2 first, and then add another seven, like this:

7 x 2 = 14
14 + 7 = 21

So, 7 x 3 = 21.

With the three times table, the sum of the numbers in the total will always add up to either three, six or nine. You can use that rule to double-check your answer fits.

In the above example, the answer is 21, and 2 + 1 = 3, so it looks like everything checks out!

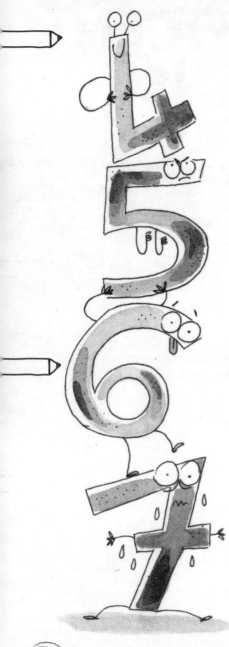

FOUR TIMES TABLE

If you're struggling to multiply a number by four, try multiplying the number by two and then two again.

For example, 8 x 4 is the same as 8 x 2 x 2.

8 x 2 = 16
16 x 2 = 32

So, 8 x 4 = 32.

The answer should always be an even number, so if it's odd, you need to try again!

SIX TIMES TABLE

The five times table is much easier than the six times table, so use your fives to help you. To multiply a number by six, multiply it first by five and then add the original number to the total.

So, 7 x 6 is the same as 7 x 5 + 7.

7 x 5 = 35
35 + 7 = 42

So, 7 x 6 = 42.

SEVEN TIMES TABLE

Because 2 + 5 = 7, you can use both the two and five times tables to work out those tricky sevens.

Here's how it would work with 8 x 7.

8 x 2 = 16 and 8 x 5 = 40
16 + 40 = 56

So, 8 x 7 = 56.

EIGHT TIMES TABLE

To multiply any number by eight, just double the number three times.

For example, 6 x 8 can be worked out like this:

Double 6 to get 12.
Double the 12 to get 24.
Then double the 24 to get 48.

So, 6 x 8 = 48.

NINE TIMES TABLE

For the nine times table, you can use an extra tool to help you – your hands!

Hold your hands up with both palms facing you and your fingers spread wide. The thumb on your left hand is number one, your left index finger is two, and so on until you reach your right thumb which is ten.

To multiply any number by nine, fold that finger down. The number of fingers to the left of the folded finger are the tens, and the number of fingers to the right of the folded finger are the units.

For example, if you want to do 3 x 9, fold down finger number three (see illustration below). This leaves your thumb and index finger to the left. That means you have two tens, which makes 20. The number of fingers to the right is seven, so you have seven units. Two tens plus seven units is 27.

So, 3 x 9 = 27.

Now try it with 4 x 9. Fold down finger number four. You'll have three fingers on the left (so three tens) and six fingers on the right (so six units). Three tens plus six units is 36.

So, 4 x 9 = 36.

Try it with some other numbers. You'll find it works each time!

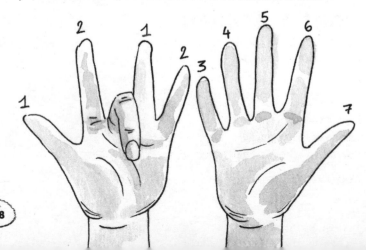

Rhyme time

This little rhyme will ensure you never forget this awesome trick:

Nasty nines are fine and fun,
Just fold down your fingers and thumbs.

ELEVEN TIMES TABLE

The first nine sums of the eleven times table are easy, as you simply repeat the number you're multiplying by, like this:

1 x 11 = 11
2 x 11 = 22
3 x 11 = 33
4 x 11 = 44
5 x 11 = 55

... and so on. But did you know there's a trick for working out the later ones, too? Here's how it works:

12 x 11
Take the 1 and 2 from 12, and add them together.
1 + 2 = 3
Now insert the 3 between the 1 and the 2, and you're left with the answer: 132.

If the two digits add up to a two-digit number, insert the second digit and add the first, like this:

75 x 11
Take the 7 and 5 from 75, and add them together.
7 + 5 = 12
Insert the 2 between the 7 and 5, leaving you with 725.
Now add the 1 onto the first digit, and you have your answer: 825.

Try it out with some other numbers!

TWELVE TIMES TABLE

For the twelve times table, you can use a couple of much simpler times tables to help you: the ten times table and the two times table.

Here's how to do it with 7 x 12:

7 x 12 is the same as 7 x 10 + 7 x 2 (so, 70 + 14)
70 + 14 = 84

So, 7 x 12 = 84.

THE TIMES-TABLE RHYME

With the tips from this chapter on your side you'll be a Multiplication Master in no time! All you have to do is remember them.

Rhyme time

Here's a rhyme to help you keep all of those times table tricks in mind:

To multiply by two, just double,
To find the threes, you treble.
Four is double, and double again,
Five you just take half of ten.
Times by five, add one for sixes,
For sevens, take five, then two again.
Everyone should know what eight is,
That's right: double, double, double.
Fold fingers for nine, no trouble,
And for multiples of ten?
Move the numbers one to the left.
Eleven's simple – write it twice,
Using two and ten for twelves is nice.

FRACTIONS

A fraction is part of a whole number. A half or ½ and a third or ⅓ are examples of fractions. You'll see that fractions are written as two numbers, with one on top of the other. The number on top is called the numerator and the number at the bottom is called the denominator.

The numerator shows you how many parts you have, and the denominator shows you how many parts the whole number is divided into.

So, if you have two-thirds or ⅔, you know that the whole number has been divided into three parts, and you have two of them.

How to remember

To remember that the numerator is the number at the top and the denominator is the number at the bottom, think of this phrase:

*Numerator **up**, denominator **down**.*

DIVIDING WITH FRACTIONS

You may find yourself faced with a sum that involves dividing by a fraction. It may seem terrifying, but there's a trick to dealing with it. Take the bottom number of the fraction (the denominator), and multiply by it instead of dividing.

For example, with the sum $10 \div \frac{1}{4}$, take the fraction and turn it into $\frac{4}{1}$.

$10 \times 4 = 40$

So, $10 \div \frac{1}{4} = 40$.

Rhyme time

This rhyme will help to remind you of the method:

Take the number you're dividing by,
Turn it upside-down and multiply.

PERCENTAGES

A percentage is a way of showing the amount of any number as part of one hundred. A half or $\frac{1}{2}$ is the same as 50 out of 100, so written as 50%. A quarter or $\frac{1}{4}$ is the same as 25 out of 100, so is written as 25%.

How to remember

Here are two ways of remembering that a percentage relates to 100:

*Per**cent**ages are like **cent**uries (which have 100 years).*

Or ...

*Per**cent**ages are like **cent**ipedes (which have 100 legs).*

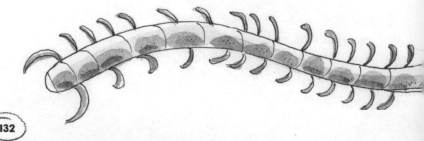

DECIMALS

Decimals are another way of writing fractions. When written as a decimal, a half or ½ is written as 0.5. A quarter or ¼ is written as 0.25. The first number to the right of the decimal point shows tenths of a whole number, and the next number shows hundredths. So, with 0.25, you have two-tenths and five-hundredths.

How to remember

The 'deci' part of the word decimal means 'ten', so think of a cake divided into ten equal slices. If the whole cake is one, then half of that cake would be 0.5, or five slices.

Divide Each Cake Into a DECImal – ten.

MEAN, MEDIAN AND MODE

There are three different ways of working out the average of a set of numbers.

With **mean** you add up all the numbers in the group together, then divide that total by how many numbers there were. So, if the group of numbers is 5, 6, 9, 10 and 10, you add the numbers together and divide by five (as there are five numbers).

5 + 6 + 9 + 10 + 10 = 40
40 ÷ 5 = 8

So 8 is the mean number in this series.

The **median** is the middle number in a series. With the numbers 5, 6, 9, 10 and 10, the median is 9. If you have a series with two middle numbers, find the median by adding those two numbers together and dividing the total by two.

The **mode** is the number that appears most often in the series. So, with 5, 6, 9, 10 and 10, the mode is 10.

How to remember

These three phrases should help you to remember which way is which:

*Me**an** means **a**verage **n**umbers.*

*****Medi**an is the **medi**um number.*

*****Mo**de appears **mo**st often.*

Rhyme time

If your memory needs an extra nudge, try using this rhyme:

Middle median, mostly mode,
A **mean** old **add**er,
And a big green toad.

SQUARE NUMBERS

When a number is multiplied by itself, it is called a square number. So 3 squared, written as 3^2, means 3 x 3, which is 9.

How to remember

Picture a flat square. Because it is flat, it has two dimensions, also known as 2D. This should help you to remember that a square number has two numbers to multiply.

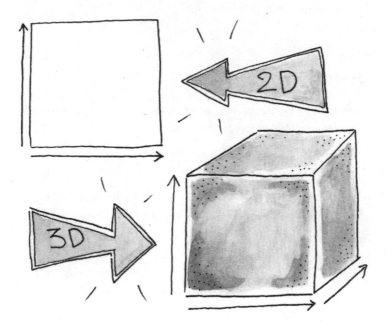

CUBE NUMBERS

A cube number has three numbers to multiply. So 3 cubed, written as 3^3, means 3 x 3 x 3, which is 27.

How to remember

Picture a 3D cube. Its three dimensions should remind you that a cubed number has three numbers to multiply.

ROOT NUMBERS

The opposite of a squared or cubed number (see page 135) is the square root ($\sqrt{}$) or cube root ($\sqrt[3]{}$). The root number is the number that was originally squared or cubed. For example, the square root of 9 is 3 (because $3 \times 3 = 9$) and the cube root of 64 is 4 (because $4 \times 4 \times 4 = 64$).

How to remember

Remember the route (root!) you used.

ROUNDING NUMBERS

When rounding to the nearest whole number, you should look at the number to the right of the decimal point.

If the number to the right of the decimal point is lower than 5, you should round down. For example, 3.4 would be rounded down to 3.

If the number to the right of the decimal point is 5 or higher, you should round up. So 3.5 would be rounded up to 4.

How to remember

Five or higher goes up, so imagine your teacher giving you a high five for getting it right!

PRIME NUMBERS

Prime numbers are numbers that can only be divided by themselves and the number 1. Examples of prime numbers are: 2, 3, 5, 7, 11, 13, 17, 19, 23, 29, 31, 37, 41, and the list goes on.

How to remember

Learning these rules should help you to work out which numbers are prime numbers:

- 0 and 1 are not prime numbers.

- Number 2 is the only even prime number.

- No numbers ending in 0 or 5 are prime, apart from 5 itself.

- If the sum of a number's digits can be divided by 3, it's not a prime number.

To remember what a prime number is, think of this phrase:

*I am pr**1**me because I can only be divided by **1** and **me**.*

CARDINAL AND ORDINAL NUMBERS

Cardinal numbers are used for counting. This means they tell you how many of something there are. For example, 1, 2, 3 or 4.

Ordinal numbers, on the other hand, show the position of something on a list. For example, 1st, 2nd, 3rd or 4th.

How to remember

Just bear in mind those initial letters:

***C**ardinal numbers are for **c**ounting.*

***O**rdinal numbers tell you the **o**rder.*

FACTORS

A whole number that divides into another whole number, with nothing left over, is a factor. For example, the factors of 6 are 1, 2, 3 and 6, because 6 can be divided by each of those numbers.

How to remember

Remember this **fact**: some numbers can be divided by many **fact**ors.

MULTIPLES

A multiple of a number can be divided by that number, with no remainder left over. Multiples of 6, for example, are 6, 12, 18 and 24. They are all numbers found in the six times table.

How to remember

Just think of multiples this way: you **multipl**y to find a **multipl**e.

POSITIVE AND NEGATIVE NUMBERS

Think of a line of numbers, all written down in order, with zero in the middle. It would look like this:

$$-5 \quad -4 \quad -3 \quad -2 \quad -1 \quad 0 \quad 1 \quad 2 \quad 3 \quad 4 \quad 5$$

Positive numbers are all the numbers written to the right of the zero. Negative numbers have a negative symbol before them (–) and fall to the left of the zero.

How to remember

If you have to multiply positive (+) and negative (–) numbers, it's helpful to think of positive numbers as the heroes and negative numbers as the villains.

If a good thing (+) happens to a hero (+), that's good (+).
So, 8 x 8 = 64.

If a good thing (+) happens to a villain (–), that's bad (–).
So, 8 x –8 = –64.

If a bad thing (–) happens to a hero (+), that's bad (–).
So, –8 x 8 = –64.

If a bad thing (–) happens to a villain (–), that's good (+).
So, –8 x –8 = 64.

Two wrongs don't usually make a right, but in this case they do!

COORDINATES

Coordinates (for example 3,1) are numbers used when plotting graphs or finding a location on a map. They tell you where to position a point on the graph, using an X-axis (along the bottom, horizontally) and a Y-axis (along the side, vertically).

On the map below, the treasure chest is at the coordinate 3,1. To find it, you just go three along on the X-axis and one up on the Y-axis. Congratulations – you're rich!

How to remember

To find 3,1, you know to go along and up, but remembering which one is which can be tricky.

To remember that the X coordinate is always written first, just keep in mind that X comes before Y in the alphabet.

To remember that the X-axis is the horizontal one and the Y-axis is vertical, just think of an X being **a cross** and it goes **across** the page.

CONVERSIONS

While the USA uses the imperial system (feet and miles) to measure length, most of Europe favours the metric system (metres and kilometres). In Great Britain, it's not unusual to see examples of either system. So it's useful to be able to remember a way to convert from one to the other.

How to remember

1 mile = 1.60934 kilometres (km), which is usually rounded down to 1.6 km. This rhyme will help you with the maths:

Miles to kilometres, ain't it great,
Just divide by five and times by eight.

1 inch = 2.54 centimetres (cm), which is rounded down to 2.5 cm. To remember this, think of a ruler. Most rulers have 12 inches on one side and 30 cm on the other: 12 x 2.5 = 30.

PARALLEL LINES

Parallel lines are lines that always remain the same distance apart and never meet. Perhaps you've seen the parallel bars in gymnastics, which are parallel to each other?

How to remember

Look at the double letter 'l' in the middle of the word 'parallel'. The two letters are, themselves, parallel lines.

PERPENDICULAR LINES

Perpendicular lines meet at an angle of 90 degrees.

How to remember

Look at the upper case 'E's in the word 'P**E**RP**E**NDICULAR'. The horizontal lines meet the vertical line at an angle of 90 degrees, so they are perpendicular.

TACKLING TRICKY SUMS

If complex sums make you break out in a cold sweat, you're not alone! Fortunately, there is a memory trick that should come as a big help. It's called 'BODMAS'.

How to remember

The letters in **BODMAS** stand for:

Brackets

Order

Division

Multiplication

Addition

Subtraction

How it works

BODMAS explains the order in which you should tackle the different parts of a complicated sum.

Let's say you're given the following sum, for example:

$2 + 18 \div 6 \times (12 \div 4)^2 - 1$

It looks impossible, but by using BODMAS you can break it down into smaller, simpler stages, like this:

I. **B** (Tackle the **b**rackets in the middle.)
$2 + 18 \div 6 \times (12 \div 4)^2 - 1$
becomes
$2 + 18 \div 6 \times (3)^2 - 1$

2. **O** (The **o**rder is the 'power' – in this case the ^{2} symbol.)
$2 + 18 \div 6 \times (3)^2 - 1$
becomes
$2 + 18 \div 6 \times 9 - 1$

3. **D** (Now handle the **d**ivision.)
$2 + 18 \div 6 \times 9 - 1$
becomes
$2 + 3 \times 9 - 1$

4. **M** (Next, do the **m**ultiplication.)
$2 + 3 \times 9 - 1$
becomes
$2 + 27 - 1$

5. **A** (Tackle the **a**ddition.)
$2 + 27 - 1$
becomes
$29 - 1$

6. **S** (Finally, do the **s**ubtraction.)
$29 - 1 = 28$

So, the answer is 28!

SHAPE UP

Ways to remember the lines, curves
and angles that make up shapes.

PARALLELOGRAM

A parallelogram is a shape with two pairs of parallel sides.
It looks like a squashed rectangle.

How to remember

A **parallel**ogram's opposite sides are **parallel**.

PARALLELOGRAM

RHOMBUS

Did you know?

If all four sides are the same length and
the opposite sides are parallel (making the
shape look like a squashed square rather
than a squashed rectangle), it's a special
kind of parallelogram called a rhombus.

TRAPEZIUM

A trapezium looks like a rectangle that has been squashed on just one side. It has only two parallel sides. The other two sides usually slope together. A trapezium looks a little like a rectangle disappearing off into the distance.

How to remember

If a **trap**ezium's two non-parallel sides carried on going, they would crash into one another and become **trap**ped.

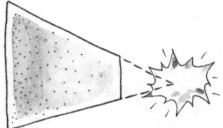

PENTAGON AND HEXAGON

A pentagon is a shape with five sides. A hexagon looks very similar to a pentagon, but it has six sides.

How to remember

The Greek word 'penta' means 'five', and also has five letters in it. A **penta**gon has **five** sides.

A h**ex**ag**on** has an **ex**tra **on**e, which makes si**x** sides all together.

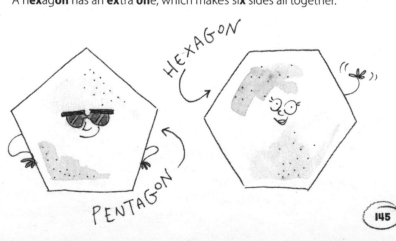

OCTAGON

An octagon is a shape with eight sides.

How to remember

An **oct**agon has **eight** sides, just like an **oct**opus has **eight** arms.

SPHERE

A sphere is a 3D circle, such as a ball or a planet.

How to remember

The Earth is a **sphere** and has an atmo**sphere**.

CYLINDER

Imagine a tube with two circles of equal size at the ends. That's a cylinder. A can of soup is a cylinder. So is the cardboard tube you get inside a roll of toilet paper.

How to remember

Think of a soup can and remember this phrase:
Cyrils's can of soup is a cylinder.

CONE

A cone has a circle or oval at one end, and a point at the other.

How to remember

Just think of the cones you often see in everyday life, such as ice-cream **cones** and traffic **cones**.

PYRAMID

Pyramids have four triangular sides that meet at a point. A pyramid normally has a square base.

How to remember

Think of the world's most famous **pyramids**: the **Pyramids** of Egypt.

CUBE

A cube is a 3D shape made up of six squares. The length, depth and width of a cube are always equal sizes.

How to remember

This one's short and sweet: just think of sugar **cubes**.

RIGHT ANGLE

If you were to stand on a spot and turn around in a full circle, you'd turn 360 degrees (written as 360°). If you do a quarter turn, that would be a 90° angle or a right angle.

Squares and rectangles have four right angles, which add up to 360°.

How to remember

Think of a capital L. An L is basically just a right angle.

OBTUSE ANGLE

An obtuse angle is an angle greater than 90° but less than 180°. The hands of a clock showing 1.45 are at an obtuse angle. A folding fan, when it has been opened up, also shows an obtuse angle.

How to remember

An **ob**tuse angle is so wide that it might **ob**struct your face, just like a fan.

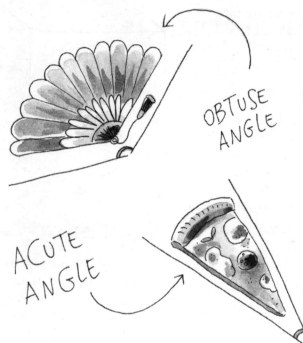

OBTUSE ANGLE

ACUTE ANGLE

ACUTE ANGLE

Any angle of less than 90° is an acute angle. The letter V is an acute angle. So is a standard slice of pizza.

How to remember

A**cute** angles are small, thin angles. You might even call them **cute**.

EQUILATERAL TRIANGLE

If all three sides of a triangle are the same length, and all three angles are 60°, it is an equilateral triangle.

How to remember

On an **equil**ateral triangle all three sides and all three angles are **equal**.

ISOSCELES TRIANGLE

An isosceles triangle has two sides and two angles of equal length and two angles of equal size.

Rhyme time

An isosceles triangle looks a bit like a Christmas tree. This reworded version of the song 'O Christmas Tree' should help you to remember that (as well as getting you in a festive mood):

Isosceles, Isosceles,
(O Christmas tree, O Christmas tree,)

Two angles have the same degrees.
(How lovely are your branches.)

Isosceles, Isosceles,
(O Christmas tree, O Christmas tree,)

You look just like a Christmas tree.
(With happiness we greet you.)

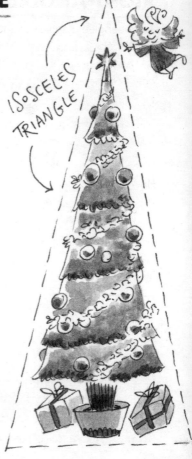

ISOSCELES TRIANGLE

SCALENE TRIANGLE

A scalene triangle is the only kind of triangle where each side and each angle is a different size. However, its angles all still add up to 180°.

How to remember
Scalene means uneven or odd. Try thinking of the uneven surface created by the **scales** of a reptile to help you remember.

RIGHT-ANGLED TRIANGLE

A right-angled triangle can also be isosceles (with two sides of equal length and two angles of equal size) or scalene (with each side and angle a different length and size). However, it is only a right-angled triangle that has a 90° angle in one corner.

The longest side of a right-angled triangle is always directly opposite the right angle. This side is called the hypotenuse.

How to remember
What is the longest side of a right-angled triangle? Just **use** the hypoten**use**.

HYPOTENUSE

90°

RIGHT-ANGLED TRIANGLE

Did you know?
There are many different types of triangle and they all have three sides, but they also have something else in common: their three angles always add up to 180°.

AREA

Area is the space inside a flat, two-dimensional shape, such as a square or rectangle.

How to remember

Are**a** is always **two**-dimensional. To remember that, just keep in mind those **two 'a**'s.

How it works

The method you should use to find a shape's area depends on what kind of shape you're looking at.

To find the area of a square or rectangle, just multiply the length by the height. To find the area of a triangle, multiply the length of the base by the height, then divide the answer by two. For a circle, you need to multiply the circle's radius by itself, then multiply that number by pi. To find about more about radius, see page 154. For more on pi, see page 155.

Rhyme time

If all of those calculations seem like a lot to take in, this rhyme should make it a lot easier.

For a rectangle or a square,
Use length times width and you are there.
For a triangle it's base times height,
Cut the number in half to get it right.
Circles are tricky, but don't be scared,
It's just pi times the radius, squared.

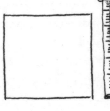

PERIMETER

The perimeter of a shape is the total measurement around its edge or rim. So, if a rectangle has a length of 15 cm and a width of 5 cm, its perimeter is 15 + 5 + 15 + 5 = 40 cm.

How to remember

Just think: pe**rim**eter.

VOLUME

Volume is the space inside a three-dimensional shape. Imagine if you had a cube-shaped swimming pool and filled it with water. The amount of water that pool can contain is its volume.

To find a shape's volume, multiply its area (see page 152) by its depth. So, to calculate the volume of a cube or cuboid, first work out the area of one of its flat faces by multiplying its length by its height. Then times that number by its depth.

The same rule applies to more complicated shapes such as cylinders. First, find the area of the circle at one end of the cylinder. Then multiply the area by the cylinder's depth.

How to remember

Volume Equals Area Times Depth can be remembered with:
Violent Eagles Are Terribly Dangerous

RADIUS

A circle's radius is the distance from its centre to its edge.

How to remember

Imagine the circle as the wheel of a bike. The radius is one of the spokes, going from the middle to the edge.

Spokes **radi**ate along the **radi**us.

DIAMETER

The diameter of a circle is its width from the edge, through the centre, to the opposite edge.

How to remember

The **d**iameter is **d**ouble the length of the radius.

CIRCUMFERENCE

Circumference is the distance around a circle. To measure a circle's circumference, multiply its diameter by pi (3.14).

How to remember

Only a **circ**le has a **circ**umference.

To remember how to work out the circumference, just think:

Cherry **pi**e is **d**elicious.
Circumference = **pi** x **d**iameter.

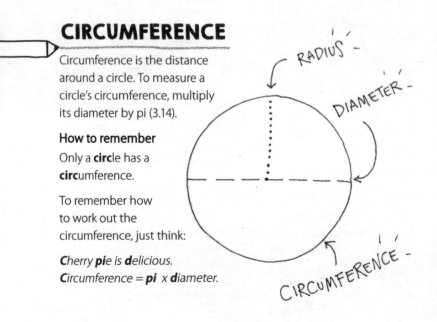

PI

Pi (often shown as the symbol π) is the name given in maths to the number 3.14. Pi has its own name because it's what you get if you divide any circle's circumference by its diameter (see page 154). You can also use pi to work out the area of any circle (see page 152).

How to remember

It's as *easy as pi* to work out the area of a circle. You just need to know that pi = 3.14.

If you forget that pi is 3.14, just remember that 3 + 1 = 4.

Rhyme time

3.14 is pi rounded to two decimal places, but the actual number goes on forever. Scientists have worked it out to over 60 trillion decimal places, and it doesn't stop there.

Here's a clever rhyme you could use to memorize the first 20 decimal places. The number of letters in each word matches the number at each decimal place.

Now, I wish I could recollect pi, "Eureka", cried the great inventor. Christmas pudding, Christmas pie, Is the problem's very centre.

(3.14159265358979323846)

'Eureka' is a reference to Archimedes, who you can find out all about on page 112.

AWESOME ART

Ways to remember some arty facts.

ART ERAS

The history of art is often divided up into different eras. These eras are known for their own distinct art styles, which were developed by the artists of the time.

Here are some of the best-known art eras:

Prehistoric

Prehistoric art was made by early people from around 70,000 BCE. The humans of this period created incredible cave paintings, often showing hunting scenes and large animals of the time. Some of the most important surviving examples of prehistoric art can be found in the Lascaux Cave in France, which contains around 600 paintings.

Ancient

Ancient art dates back to the ancient cultures and societies of places including China, India, Greece and Rome. Roman frescoes (wall murals) and ancient Greek vases are examples of this art era.

Middle Ages

Art from the Middle Ages, also known as Medieval art, often has a strong religious influence. Many of the most valuable pieces of art from this period can now be found in churches and cathedrals.

Renaissance

Renaissance is a French word that means 'rebirth'. However, Renaissance art refers mainly to the great works of art that were created in Europe during the 14th, 15th and 16th centuries. Famous artists of the Renaissance era include Michelangelo, Leonardo da Vinci and Raphael.

Baroque

The Baroque era was at its peak in the 17th century. Baroque paintings and sculptures are often recognizable from their dramatic (and sometimes sinister) style. Great Baroque artists include Peter Paul Rubens, Rembrandt and Caravaggio.

Romanticism

Romanticism was at its height during the late 18th century and first half of the 19th century. The 'romantic' part refers not to love, but to a general artistic shift towards feelings and emotions. Well-known artists of the Romantic era include John Constable, J. M. W. Turner and William Blake. Art from this period often featured sweeping landscapes.

Turn the page to discover some other art eras and how to remember them.

Impressionism

Artists of this 19th-century era painted scenes as if they had caught just a glimpse of them. Famous Impressionists include Claude Monet, Pierre-Auguste Renoir and Paul Cézanne.

Pop Art

The Pop Art era emerged during the 1950s. Pop artists such as Andy Warhol and Roy Lichtenstein were influenced by modern objects and themes such as soup cans and comic strips.

How to remember

Use the sentence below to remember the art eras in order.

*Painting **A**rt **M**ay **R**eally **B**reak **R**ules = **I**nteresting **P**ictures!*
*(**P**rehistoric, **A**ncient, **M**iddle Ages, **R**enaissance, **B**aroque, **R**omanticism, **I**mpressionism, **P**op Art.)*

GREAT PAINTINGS

The history of art is packed with incredible masterpieces. The poem below should help with getting to grips with the artists behind some of the most famous works of art.

Rhyme time

Vincent van Gogh's Sunflowers,
Show off the Dutchman's powers.
While da Vinci's Mona Lisa,
Is certainly sure to please ya!
Michelangelo's Sistine ceiling,
Shows true artistic feeling,
And Gustav Klimt's The Kiss,
Is a painting not to miss.
The Scream by Edvard Munch,
Is the fifth painting in this bunch.
While Andy Warhol's
Campbell's Soup,
Finishes this famous group.

THE COLOUR WHEEL

The colour wheel isn't just any old colourful wheel – it's a tool that shows how colours work and how to mix colours together to make new ones.

Red, yellow and blue are the three primary colours. They can't be made by mixing any other colours together. However, all other colours can be made by mixing different combinations of primary colours together.

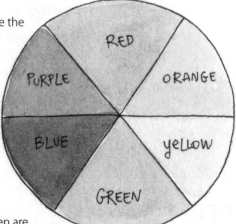

Purple, orange and green are the secondary colours. They can be created by mixing together the two primary colours on either side of them on the wheel.

So, purple is made by mixing blue and red. Orange is made by mixing red and yellow. Green is made by mixing yellow and blue.

Rhyme time

When you don't have a colour wheel handy, this rhyme will help you to remember which colours are primary and which colours are secondary:

First came red and yellow, with their best friend blue,
Then came green and orange, and purple came along too.

MIGHTY MUSIC

Ways to remember how music gets from the page to your ears.

MUSICAL NOTES

When learning how to read and play music, one of the most useful things to remember is the alphabet. Musical notes are named after the first seven letters: A, B, C, D, E, F and G.

How to remember

Just picture those seven letters being repeated on the white keys of a piano, like this:

STAVE

When you look at music written down, you'll see that the musical notes are written as a series of dots on top of five parallel lines. This set of five lines is called a stave.

How to remember

There are five lines in a stave and five letters in the word 'stave'.

TREBLE CLEF

The symbol drawn at the bottom of this page is called a treble clef. When looking at written music, you'll often see a treble clef on the left-hand side.

Musical instruments that have a high sound (such as violins and recorders) use the notes shown next to the treble clef. The higher notes played on a piano, using the pianist's right hand, are also shown next to a treble clef.

Starting from the bottom, the notes that appear on each line of a piece of music using a treble clef are: E, G, B, D and F.

The notes that appear in the spaces between each line, from the bottom, are: F, A, C and E.

How to remember

For the notes that appear on the lines, use **E**very **G**ood **B**oy **D**eserves **F**ruit.

Rhyme time

For the notes between the lines, try this rhyme:

*A note in a space, Is as plain as your **FACE**.*

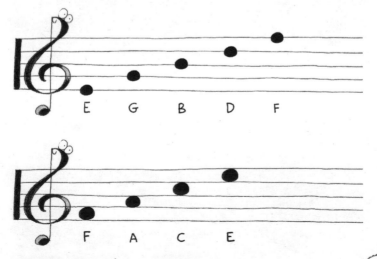

BASS CLEF

The symbol on the left of the lines below is a bass clef. It's used in a similar way to a treble clef (see page 161), but by intruments that have a low sound, such as a tuba or cello. The lower notes played on a piano, using the pianist's left hand, are also shown next to a bass clef.

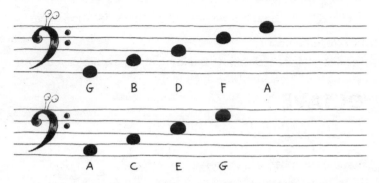

Running from the bottom line to the top, the notes that appear on each line of a piece of music using a bass clef are: G, B, D, F and A.

The notes that appear in the spaces between each line, from the bottom, are: A, C, E and G.

How to remember

For the notes that appear on the lines, think of: **G**ood **B**urgers **D**eserve **F**ries **A**lways.

For the notes between the lines, try: **A**ll **C**ats **E**at **G**oldfish.

TONIC

Eight notes played in order make a scale, and the first note in a scale is called the tonic.

Different scales have different names, depending on what their tonic is. If the tonic is C, for example, the scale is the C major scale. The notes in this scale, in order, are: C, D, E, F, G, A, B and C.

How to remember
The first note of a scale always sounds right, like a **tonic** for your ears.

OCTAVE

The eight notes in a scale make up an octave. In the C major scale shown above in the tonic section, C is both the first and last note. However, the C at the beginning is lower than the C at the end. These two notes are at either end of the octave.

How to remember
When a word starts with 'oct', it often means that it has eight of something. An **oct**opus has eight arms, an **oct**agon has eight sides and an **oct**ave has eight notes.

SEMITONE

A semitone sounds halfway between one note and the next. The C major scale mentioned above is the simplest scale, because you do not need to sharpen (raise) or flatten (lower) the notes. The notes are all 'natural'.

Scales that start on other notes need sharps and flats (see page 164) to make them sound right. A sharp note is a semitone higher than a natural note. A flat note is a semitone lower than a natural note.

How to remember
'Semi' means half. A **semi**-circle is half a circle. A **semi**-detached house takes up half of a building. A **semi**tone is half a note.

SHARPS

A sharp is shown on a piece of written music as a symbol that looks a little like a hashtag (like this: #). When you see this symbol next to the clef, it changes the sound of the note to a fifth higher than the line or space the note appears on.

The first scale that has a sharp added to it is G major. It has an F#. G is a fifth higher than C (the five notes from C to G – C, D, E, F and G – are a fifth). When you go up another fifth, to the D major scale, you need two sharps – F# and C#.

A sharp is added to scales each time in this order: F#, C#, G#, D#, A#, E# and B#.

How to remember

The order of those sharps can be remembered with:

Father Charles Goes Down And Ends Battle.

FLATS

The symbol for a flat looks a little like a lower-case letter b (♭). When you see this symbol next to the clef, it changes the sound of the note to a fourth lower than the line or space the note appears on.

The first scale with a flat is F major, which contains a B♭. The next scale with a flat is B♭ major, with two flats, then E♭ with three flats, and so on.

Flats are added to scales in this order: B♭, E♭, A♭, D♭, G♭, C♭ and F♭.

How to remember

Remember the order of the flats with:

Battle Ends And Down Goes Charles's Father.

PARTS OF AN ORCHESTRA

An orchestra is a large group of musicians who play lots of different musical instruments together. Orchestras are often made up of four types of instruments: string (such as violins and cellos), percussion (instruments that are hit or shaken, such as xylophones and drums), woodwind (including flutes and oboes) and brass (such as trumpets and trombones).

How to remember

Remember **s**tring, **p**ercussion, **w**oodwind and **b**rass with this phrase:

Symphonies **p**layed **w**ith **b**rilliance.

Did you know?

A symphony is a long piece of music that has been written specifically for an orchestra to play. A symphony usually has four sections, which are known as movements.

ORCHESTRA INSTRUMENTS

An orchestra can have around 100 musicians, all playing instruments in different sections (see page 165 to find out more about the various parts of an orchestra).

The memory tricks below will help you remember some of the most common instruments that make up an orchestra.

How to remember

For the string instruments, use this phrase:

***Viola**'s **violin** said, '**Cello**' to the **double bass**.*

The brass section often includes a horn and three instruments beginning with 't' (tuba, trumpet and trombone), so you could think of this phrase:

*The drinking **horn** held three **teas** (**t**'s).*

For the woodwind instruments, try memorizing this handy rhyme:

***Clarinet**, **oboe** and **bassoon**,
Piccolo, **flute** and **saxophone**.*

For the percussion instruments, call to mind the very odd character here, which has a drum for a head, cymbals for eyes, a tambourine nose and a triangle for a mouth.

THE BEST OF THE REST

Ways to remember lots of other useful things.

THE CLASSICAL GREEK ALPHABET

The classical Greek alphabet has 24 letters, from Alpha to Omega. Letters from the Greek alphabet come up in English more often than you might think, particularly in maths and science. For example, gamma radiation takes its name from a Greek letter, and the word 'alpha' is often used to mean the best or brightest.

Rhyme time

This rhyming tongue-twister lists every letter of the classical Greek alphabet in order:

This is Greek and how they spelt her,
***Alpha**, **Beta**, **Gamma**, **Delta**,*
***Epsilon**, **Zeta**,*
***Eta**, **Theta**,*
*Then **Iota**, **Kappa** too,*
*Followed up by **Lambda**, **Mu**.*

***Nu**, **Xi**,*
***Omicron**, **Pi**,*
*After that, **Rho**, **Sigma**, **Tau**,*
***Upsilon**, **Phi**, and still three more,*
***Chi**, **Psi** and **Omega** makes twenty-four.*

LEFT AND RIGHT

If you find it hard to tell your left from you right, don't worry. There are some *handy* memory tricks to help.

How to remember

Hold your hands out in front of you, with your palms down and your thumbs sticking out. You'll see that your left hand makes an 'L' shape – as in, **L** for **Left**.

If you're right-handed, you could also use this phrase:

*I **write** with my **right**, and what's **left** is my **left**.*

Another way is to give yourself a visual aid. For example, if you like to wear a watch or a bracelet, you could always wear it on your left wrist as a secret reminder to yourself.

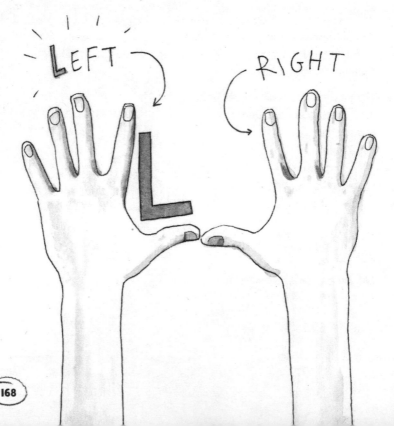

OPENING AND UNSCREWING

Whether you're opening a jar, turning a screw or even replacing a light bulb, you nearly always turn them anticlockwise (to the left) to loosen or open, and clockwise (to the right) to tighten or close.

How to remember

Just think of this easy phrase:

Lefty **loose**y,
Righty **tight**y.

BICYCLE BRAKES

When you're riding a bike, it's important to know how to stop. You probably already know that squeezing the brake levers by the handlebars will bring the bike to a halt, but did you know that each lever works a different brake?

The right brake is for the front wheel and the left brake is for the rear wheel. It's important that you use the left brake first to stop the rear wheel. If you squeeze the right brake first, you'll be in danger of going flying over the handlebars.

On top of all that, you need to remember to keep your gaze ahead of you on the road. If you look down, you'll probably start to wobble and lose your balance!

How to remember

When you're out on your bike, always keep in mind:

Left before right,
Don't look down!

TIE A TIE

Don't get yourself tied up in knots when you're trying to get ready for school in the morning. To master your tie-tying skills, just try out the tricks below.

How to remember

Imagine the wide side of the tie is a rabbit and the narrow side is a fence. To tie your tie, take the rabbit over the fence, then under the fence. Finally, bring the rabbit up through the middle, then down through the loop you have made – and you're done!

If all that rabbit stuff leaves you scratching your head, you could simply learn:

Over, under, around and through.

PORT AND STARBOARD

Port means the left side of the ship and starboard means the right side.

Rhyme time

Think of the number of letters in the two words. Both 'port' and 'left' have four letters. Both 'starboard' and 'right' have more than four.

Port and left have letters four,
Starboard and right both have more.

ONE FOR SORROW, TWO FOR JOY

If you are superstitious, you might believe that different numbers mean different things. Lots of people have their own lucky number, while many regard the number 13 to be unlucky. Some people even think that specific numbers of magpies grouped together have various meanings.

Rhyme time

The poem below is easy to learn and explains the superstitious meaning behind each number of magpies:

One for sorrow, two for joy,
Three for a girl, four for a boy,
Five for silver, six for gold,
Seven for a secret never to be told,
Eight for a wish, nine for a kiss,
Ten for a bird you must not miss.

LIFE-SAVING

If you are ever in the situation of having to help someone who is unconscious while waiting for an ambulance, there are three stages you can learn that could really help.

1. Make sure the person's airway is open by tilting their chin back a little. Also check to make sure nothing is blocking their mouth and throat.

2. Look for signs of breathing. Can you see the person's chest rising and falling? Can you hear them breathing or can you feel their breath? If you have a mirror, you could try holding it just in front of the person's mouth. If they are breathing, the mirror will steam up a little.

3. Check the person's circulation. By feeling for a pulse in their neck or wrist, you can make sure that their heart is beating.

How to remember

Learning all of the above is as simple as **ABC**:

Airway
Breathing
Circulation

SURVIVAL

When you go away on a trip or holiday, you might like to pack all sorts of clothes, toys and books in your bag. However, there are actually only three things that are truly essential for survival:

1. Shelter – to provide protection against the weather

2. Water – because your body needs to stay hydrated

3. Food – to prevent you from losing your energy and ultimately starving

How to remember

If you have those things you can *Survive Without Fear*! (**S**helter, **W**ater, **F**ood.)

It's also useful to remember the number three. You cannot survive longer than:

- Three minutes without oxygen

- Three hours at freezing temperatures

- Three days without water

- Three weeks without food

DECATHLON

A decathlon is a sporting contest where athletes compete across ten different events.

How to remember

To remember all ten events, it helps to break them down into smaller groups, like this:

- Three runs (100 metres, 400 metres, 1500 metres)

- Three jumps (long jump, high jump, pole vault)

- Three throws (discus, javelin, shot put)

Remember all nine of those events and you'll have no problem getting over the last **hurdle**. The 110-metre **hurdle**s, to be precise – because that's the tenth event.

SIGNS OF THE ZODIAC

There are 12 signs of the western zodiac. Each sign represents a group of stars in the sky and is symbolized by an animal or object (which you can see on the page opposite).

Astrologers are people who believe that people's lives are influenced by the positions of these groups of stars on the day they were born. That is why you have a star sign. If you don't know your star sign, you can find it in the table below:

Star Sign	Symbol	Birthdate
Aries	The Ram	21 March–19 April
Taurus	The Bull	20 April–20 May
Gemini	The Twins	21 May–21 June
Cancer	The Crab	22 June–22 July
Leo	The Lion	23 July–22 August
Virgo	The Maiden	23 August–22 September
Libra	The Scales	23 September–23 October
Scorpio	The Scorpion	24 October–21 November
Sagittarius	The Archer	22 November–21 December
Capricorn	The Goat	22 December–19 January
Aquarius	The Water Carrier	20 January–18 February
Pisces	The Fish	19 February–20 March

How to remember

To remember all 12 signs in order, just think of this phrase. The initial letters of each word match the initial letters of the star signs:

*A*ll *T*he *G*reen *C*ats *L*ike *V*ery *L*arge *S*caly *S*almon *C*anned *A*nd *P*ickled. (*A*ries, *T*aurus, *G*emini, *C*ancer, *L*eo, *V*irgo, *L*ibra, *S*corpio, *S*agittarius, *C*apricorn, *A*quarius, *P*isces.)

ARIES

TAURUS

GEMINI

CANCER

LEO

VIRGO

LIBRA

SCORPIO

SAGITTARIUS

CAPRICORN

AQUARIUS

PISCES

SETTING A TABLE

Want to impress everyone at home by showing off your knowledge of how to properly set a table? Here's how each place setting should look:

How to remember

To remember what goes where, all you have to know is your right from your left.

The word 'left' has an even number of letters, and so do the items that sit on the left (fork with four letters and napkin with six letters).

The word 'right' has an odd number of letters, and so do the items that sit on the right (knife, spoon and glass, all with five letters).

COFFEE

If you've ever looked at a coffee-shop menu, you'll know there are lots of different ways that coffee can be served with milk, foam and even chocolate. Here are some of the most popular coffee choices:

Espresso
Served in a tiny cup, this is simply a shot of pure black coffee.

Macchiato
A shot of espresso in a small cup, with a little steamed or foamed milk added in.

Americano
A shot of espresso served in a large mug and mixed with hot water.

Latte
A large cup filled with espresso and steamed milk, topped with a little foamed milk.

Cappucino
A shot of espresso topped with lots of foamed milk and sometimes chocolate sprinkles.

Mocha
A comination of espresso, steamed milk, chocolate and sometimes even whipped cream.

How to remember
To remember all six of the above coffees, just think of some wealthy meerkats!

Even Meerkats Are Late Counting Money
(Espresso, Macchiato, Americano, Latte, Cappucino, Mocha)

Notes

Why not have a go at writing your own mnemonics, rhymes
and memory aids? You will always remember your own
inventions best!

Index

Words and phrases in bold are main entries.

Remember

Recall

Remind

Recollect

Relive

Memorize

Commemorate